Act Like Men

**RANDALL J.
BREWER**

ACT LIKE MEN

CONTENTS

INTRODUCTION

We live in an age that is deeply confused about manhood. Strength is often mislabeled as toxicity, courage is mistaken for aggression, conviction is mocked as intolerance, and responsibility is avoided at all costs. At the same time, men are encouraged to be passive, emotionally driven, and spiritually disengaged - present in body, but absent in leadership. Into this confusion, the Word of God speaks with stunning clarity and authority. In 1 Cor. 16:13,14, the apostle Paul delivers a short but thunderous command to men that has echoed through the centuries, "Be watchful, stand firm in the faith, act like men, be strong. Let all you do be done with love."

In just two verses, God lays out a complete framework for biblical manhood. This is not cultural masculinity. It is not machismo. It is not domination, intimidation, or ego-driven toughness. It is God-defined manhood - manhood forged by truth, strengthened by faith, governed by love, and expressed through responsibility. The phrase "act like men" is not a casual suggestion; it is a divine mandate. It is a call to maturity. It is a summons to courage. It is a demand that men rise up from spiritual sleep and live intentionally, decisively, and sacrificially. God is not asking men to be perfect, but He is absolutely calling them to be awake, anchored, strong, and loving.

Paul begins with the command to be watchful. A biblical man is not careless, distracted, or unaware. He understands that life is a battlefield, not a playground. Spiritual danger is real. Temptation is constant. Deception is subtle. A man who acts like a man learns to stay alert to his own heart, to the needs of his family, to the schemes of the enemy, and to the direction of God. Watchfulness means a man guards what enters his mind, what shapes his values, and what influences his decisions. He does not drift through life reacting to circumstances; he lives intentionally, eyes open, spirit engaged. A watchful man prays, discerns, and prepares. He understands that what he ignores today may destroy him tomorrow.

Next, Paul commands all men to stand firm in the faith. Biblical manhood is rooted in conviction. A man who acts like a man does not shift with cultural winds or bow to pressure. He stands on truth even when it is unpopular, costly, or misunderstood. Standing fast does not mean being harsh or arrogant - it means being anchored. A godly man knows what he believes, why he believes it, and whom he has believed. His faith is not inherited, borrowed, or shallow; it is tested, personal, and resilient. He remains faithful in trials, faithful in temptation, faithful in obscurity, and faithful in success. The world desperately needs men who will not compromise their faith for comfort or convenience - men who stand when others sit, speak when others remain silent, and obey God when obedience is hard.

Paul then declares that all men must act like men and be strong. This phrase speaks directly to courage, resolve, and inner strength. Biblical strength is not measured by physical power alone, but by moral backbone, spiritual endurance, and emotional discipline. A man who acts like a man takes faces challenges head-on. He confronts sin in his own life before addressing it in others. He endures hardship, resists temptation, and perseveres when quitting would be easier. True strength is the ability to stand when you feel weak, to lead when you feel inadequate, and to do what is right when it costs you something. Godly strength is not loud or showy; it is steady, faithful, and dependable.

Finally, Paul anchors manhood with the crucial command to walk in love at all times. Strength without love becomes cruelty. Courage without compassion becomes oppression. Biblical manhood is not complete unless it is governed by love. A man who acts like a man loves sacrificially. He loves his wife with patience and honor. He loves his children with instruction and consistency. He loves others with grace, humility, and mercy. His leadership is not about control, but about service. His authority is expressed through responsibility, not entitlement. Walking in love is choosing to put others before self. It is remaining faithful when feelings fluctuate. It is reflecting the heart of Christ in everyday life.

"Act Like Men" is a call to rise above passivity, confusion, and compromise. It is an invitation to rediscover what God intended men to be: alert, anchored, courageous, strong, and loving. This book is not written to condemn men, but to challenge them - to call them higher, deeper, and stronger in their walk with God. If you are tired of drifting, if you are weary of half-hearted faith, if you sense God calling you to more, then this book is for you. The world does not need louder men -

it needs stronger men. Men who will watch. Men who will stand. Men who will be strong. Men who will love. It is time to rise. It is time to live with purpose. It is time to act like men.

| 1 |

"MEN MATTER"

M en matter. Godly men are anchors in a drifting culture. They stand when others bow, speak truth when silence is easier, and choose obedience when compromise is applauded. A godly man may never stand on a stage or make headlines, but heaven records every quiet act of obedience, every unseen sacrifice, and every faithful prayer. Scripture reminds us that God works through men who are willing, not perfect. Noah mattered when he built an ark in a world that mocked him. Joseph mattered when he resisted temptation in private. David mattered when he chose courage over comfort. Nehemiah mattered when he rebuilt what others had abandoned. Their greatness was not in their reputation - it was in their obedience. Godly men matter because they shape homes, churches, and nations. A godly man protects what God entrusts to him - his heart, his family, his integrity, and his faith. A man who chooses righteousness plants seeds that generations will harvest long after he's gone.

The enemy works hard to silence godly men through discouragement, distraction, shame, and isolation because he knows the power a submitted man carries. But God is still calling men to rise, not in arrogance, but in humility; not in dominance, but in devotion; not in anger, but in authority rooted in love and truth. If you are a godly man striving to live right in a crooked world, you matter. Your consistency matters. Your repentance matters. Your perseverance matters. Heaven sees you even when the world overlooks you. God has not forgotten your labor, your tears, or your stand. Now is the time for godly men to stand tall - not puffed up with pride but grounded in faith. The world does not need fewer godly men; it needs more men who fear God, love truth, and live courageously. When godly men rise, darkness loses ground and hope finds a voice. All godly men matter because God still builds His kingdom through faithful men who dare to walk with Him.

We live in a world that is continually trying to erode the ground God has given men to stand on. It's our ground! God gave it to us! We can't sit idly by as the world tries to belittle our manhood. It's time for all men to rise up and act like men. Stop struggling with those things that seem to always overwhelm you. You are not just a man who believes in God, you are a man of God. That title carries weight. It carries authority. It carries responsibility. And it demands action. The world does not need more passive men, silent men, or men who know the truth but live like they don't. The world needs men who stand, men who refuse to be pushed around by fear, temptation, compromise, or the lies of the enemy. The devil is not impressed by your church attendance, your Bible on the shelf, or the prayers you meant to pray. He only respects resistance. The Bible says in James 4:7, "Resist the devil and he will flee from you." You don't negotiate with the devil or tolerate him. You stand up in godly strength and resist him.

Too many men of God are allowing the enemy to shove them into corners. They're being pushed into silence when they should speak, pushed into comfort when they should fight, pushed into fear when they've been given authority, and pushed into distraction when they've been called to purpose. Rise up and act like a man because you weren't saved to be soft, you weren't redeemed to be timid, and you weren't called to blend in. You were called to stand firm. A man of God does not let circumstances dictate his obedience. He doesn't let culture define his masculinity. He doesn't let the devil set the terms of engagement. He knows who he is, whose he is, and what he's been entrusted with. When the enemy pushes, a man of God pushes back with truth. When temptation whispers, he answers with the Word. When fear rises, he stands on faith. When the world mocks righteousness, he wears it boldly. Stop letting the devil treat you like you're weak, unsure, or defeated. You are none of those things.

There is a need in the world for strong, courageous, Christlike men who will do what is right no matter what their circumstances may be. This generation is desperate for real men who lead their homes, men who protect their integrity, and men who pray even when it's uncomfortable. They need men who refuse to quit when it gets hard. This is the type of man you are called, equipped and anointed to be. So straighten your back. Guard your heart. Renew your mind. Take your place. You're a man of God - now act like it. The world is lacking brave men who love their Savior. This is why it's time to get real, get serious, and get accountable. Hosea 6:1 says, "Come, let us return to the Lord." That means you give God first place in your life and in your home. The heroic men of times past have faded into folklore, being replaced by men who have been feminized in today's culture. Gone are the men with the courage of William Wallace, the boldness of George Patton, the ability to preach like Billy Graham.

It's time to grow up and act like men. Don't act like a woman, an animal, or a child. Act like the man God created you to be. We are living in a time when manhood is confused, mocked, softened, and redefined. The culture tells men to be passive, emotional without discipline, driven by appetite, or absent altogether. But God has never been unclear about His design for a man. The Apostle Paul issues a clear command in 1 Cor. 16:13,14, "Be watchful, stand firm in the faith, act like men, be strong. Let all you do be done in love." In plain language: Grow up. Stand firm. Be courageous. Act like men. A godly man should not act like a woman because God created men and women with distinct roles, strengths, and responsibilities. Men are the leaders of the home and scripture calls men to lead with courage, strength, responsibility, and sacrificial love, not passivity or emotional instability. When a man abandons his God-given masculine calling, he weakens his family, the church, and himself.

True biblical masculinity is not harsh or domineering, but steadfast, disciplined, protective, and accountable before God. A godly man honors women best by being fully the man God designed him to be - standing firm in truth, bearing burdens, leading with integrity, and walking in obedience, not confusion. Rise up and be the man of the house and never be like a child who avoids responsibility, reacts emotionally instead of responding wisely, and wants pleasure without discipline and comfort without commitment. There is a difference between childlike faith and childish behavior. Children want to be rescued from consequences. Mature men accept responsibility and learn from them. Children react. Mature men respond. Children chase pleasure. Mature men choose purpose. God never calls men to remain immature - He calls them to grow up. 1 Cor. 13:11 says, "When I was a child, I spoke as a child, I understood as a child, I thought as a child; but when I became a man, I put away childish things."

God is not raising spiritual infants - He is forming men who are strong and mature, men who don't live by the flesh like an animal. Animals live by instinct, hunger, lust, dominance, and fear. When a man lives only to satisfy his flesh, he lives beneath God's calling for his life. Prov. 16:32 says, "He that rules his spirit is greater than he that takes a city." Real strength is not how loud you are. Real strength is not intimidation. Real strength is self-control. A godly man controls his anger, guards his eyes, disciplines his body, and rules his spirit. The flesh wants to react while the Holy Spirit teaches a man to respond. God is not raising men who live by instinct, impulse, and appetite. He is forming men of strength, restraint, and maturity.

An animal reacts. A man reflects. An animal follows desire. A man follows truth. The flesh wants what feels good now. It craves ease, comfort, pleasure, and dominance. Men were shaped by God to be governed by conviction, not driven by emotion or impulse or fleshly urges and desires.

Where have all the good men gone? In a world loud with opinions but quiet in conviction, true strength of character has become rare. Courage is no longer measured by the willingness to stand alone, to speak truth when it costs something, or to do what is right when no one is watching. Too often, comfort has replaced commitment, and silence has taken the place of responsibility. Because of this, society as a whole is rapidly running downhill toward the cliff of doom and despair. We live in a world that is broken, confused, and flawed. It's a world that calls good evil and evil good. Sad to say, it's a world where you can't tell the difference between a man and a woman. Men act like women and women act like men. This is happening because the Christian men of this world are not rising up to become the real men God called them to be. This dereliction of duty is a dishonor to God, to our fellow brethren, and to ourselves. Good men have not vanished, but they have been distracted, discouraged, or silenced.

The world doesn't need louder men; it needs stronger ones - men of integrity, courage, and resolve who are willing to stand, lead, protect, and serve. When men rise again in character, courage will follow, and the world will feel the difference. Character is the root. Courage is the fruit. A man does not become courageous because the world applauds him. He becomes courageous because his inner life is aligned with truth, with God, with conviction, and with responsibility. When a man chooses integrity in private, strength begins to form in public. Character is forged when no one is watching. It is built in the unseen choices, by choosing truth over convenience, faithfulness over compromise, and obedience over excuses. And when character stands upright, courage is not far behind. Courage is not the absence of fear - it is the refusal to be ruled by it. A man of character stands when it would be easier to sit, speaks when silence would be safer, and leads when retreat would feel more comfortable.

When men rise again in character families feel secure, communities regain stability, churches regain authority, and nations regain strength. The world today needs men whose backbone is character and whose heartbeat is courage. The decline we see around us is not merely moral - it is relational and spiritual. And restoration will not begin in systems, politics, or policies. It will begin when men decide once again to live rightly, walk humbly with God, and lead boldly where they stand. One man of character can steady a household. A generation of courageous men can change a culture. When men rise up and become who God created them to be, the world will feel the difference, and it will never be the same again. Character counts because in the eyes of God the messenger is just as important as the message being delivered. You can't have the wrong type of person delivering God's message to the world. The absence of integrity and character in God's instrument of delivery will make the message null and void.

Trueness and honesty need to be in the heart of every true man of God, men who won't be bought or sold with fortune, fame, and power. A true man of God does not merely speak truth; he lives it, even when the cost is high and the reward is invisible. Integrity is who he is when no one is watching, and faithfulness is what remains when temptation knocks loudly. In a world where men are constantly being offered shortcuts - fortune without faith, fame without faithfulness, and power without purity - the true man of God stands unmoved. He cannot be bought, bribed, or bent. His convictions are not for sale. His loyalty belongs to God alone. Gold may glitter. Applause may roar. Authority may entice. But none of these can replace a clean heart before God. A true man of God understands that character outlives charisma, and integrity outweighs influence. He knows that success gained by compromise is failure in disguise. He would rather walk alone in truth than stand surrounded by men in deception.

In every generation, there are many who seek influence, position, and recognition but few who seek character. Godly character has always been rare, and in our day, it feels almost endangered. Yet the scarcity of such men only magnifies their value. Where godly character is absent, confusion multiplies. Where it is present, lives are steadied, families are strengthened, and communities are changed. A man of godly character is not defined by perfection, but by conviction. He stands firm when compromise is easier. He chooses truth when lies are popular. He lives the same in private as he does in public, knowing that God sees both. In a culture that rewards shortcuts and applause, a man of integrity quietly chooses obedience even when no one is watching. Character begins in the heart long before it is ever seen in outward actions. It is forged in prayer, sharpened in obedience, and proven in pressure. Such men of godly character are rare, but they are so desperately needed.

These men are absolutely essential because the world is aching for anchors. Homes need fathers whose words can be trusted. Churches need leaders whose lives back up their preaching. Communities need men whose presence brings safety, wisdom, and peace. Godly character creates stability in unstable times. It reminds others that righteousness is still possible and faithfulness still matters. Scripture shows us that when God wants to change a nation, He often begins with one man who will not bend. Noah stood righteous in a corrupt world. Joseph remained pure in a place of temptation. Daniel refused compromise in a hostile culture. None of them were common. All of them were essential. Men of godly character are rare because character is costly. It requires daily surrender, disciplined choices, and the courage to stand alone if necessary. But it is precisely this cost that makes such men so powerful. When a man fears God more than he fears man, his life becomes a testimony that cannot be ignored.

Men matter and this is why the world needs men whose strength is guided by humility, and whose authority flows from obedience to God. Though they may be few, their impact is immeasurable. Now more than ever, God is calling men to rise up in principle, honesty, and in devotion. Godly men may be rare, but when they stand, darkness retreats, hope is restored, and the next generation sees what is possible when a man chooses character over compromise. God is still searching for men who will not bow to cultural pressure, who will not dilute truth to gain acceptance, and who will not trade eternal reward for temporary gain. Men whose yes is yes, whose no is no, and whose word carries weight because it is anchored in righteousness. These are the men God entrusts with influence. These are the men heaven defends. These are the men history remembers. A true man of God is pure in intention, honest in heart, and unwavering in loyalty. He stands tall because he is a true man of God.

The world today is lacking strong, healthy, godly, vibrant, capable, confident, and courageous men. There is nothing more dangerous in this world than an insecure, ungrounded man because when a man does not know who he is, he will react instead of responding, dominate instead of leading, and destroy instead of building. Lacking inner security, he looks for worth in control, applause, or power, and when those things are threatened, fear turns into anger. An ungrounded heart is easily shaken by offense, comparison, and pride. This is what street gangs and bars are full of and why casinos grow larger and larger. Non-profit organizations are started because men don't do what God has called them to do. Wives and children suffer because some man didn't fulfill his God-given role as husband and father. The world has a lot of problems, and the solution starts with real men of God. This is why all the men of God in the world must rise up, take their stand, and act like men with true strength and conviction.

Every man, whether he admits it or not, carries a deep desire to be great. Not famous. Not powerful in the world's sense. But significant. They have a longing to matter, to leave something better than he found it, to make his life count. God planted that hunger for greatness in the heart of man. From the beginning, man was created to rule, to steward, to lead, and to build. Adam was not placed in the garden to drift, but to cultivate. He was not formed to shrink back, but to step forward. The desire to be great is a divine spark meant to drive a man toward responsibility, excellence, and impact. Jesus defined greatness in God's eyes when He said, "Whoever wants to become great among you must be your servant" (Matt. 20:26). Greatness in the kingdom of God is not measured by how many serve you, but by how many are lifted because you showed up. Great men make people stronger. They challenge those around them to rise higher, think deeper, and walk straighter not by force, but by example.

If a man is going to make a positive impact on the world, he must embrace greatness - not arrogance, not ego, but greatness of character. Jesus never lived small. David never thought small. Nehemiah never planned small. They lived submitted, obedient, and courageous lives being fully aware that God had placed greatness within them for the sake of others. Men who matter don't dominate others; they develop them. Their presence brings clarity, courage, and confidence because they live with integrity, discipline, and purpose. They speak life, set standards, and refuse to tolerate mediocrity in themselves or in others. Because of them, people stand taller, become braver, and discover strength they didn't know they had. Great men leave them stronger than they found them. Great men leave legacies of faith, courage, and integrity. God calls all men to have a strong character, to be bold and courageous, to be great in love, in courage, in faith, and in obedience. These are the men who change the world.

| 2 |

"IN THE WILDERNESS"

All men want to be great. In fact, to make a positive impact on the world, they need to be great. For that to happen, you need to love to do the things that will make you great. You can't be great unless you first put in the work to be great. In other words, no pain, no gain. Greatness is never accidental. It is forged, not gifted. Shaped, not stumbled upon. In the Kingdom of God, greatness does not come to the comfortable, the casual, or the complacent - it comes to those willing to put in the work. You cannot be great without first being willing to grow, and growth always involves pain. Every man who has ever become strong was once weak. Every servant God has ever elevated was first tested, stretched, and refined. There is no shortcut to spiritual greatness - only a narrow road marked by blood, sweat, tears, hard work, discipline, obedience, and endurance. Pain is not your enemy. Pain is your instructor. God uses discomfort to develop depth, hardship to produce humility, and resistance to build resolve.

The resistance you face is the very thing building your strength. The struggle you endure is producing perseverance. The pressure you feel is shaping character. Faith that has never been tested has never been proven. Character that has never been challenged has never been confirmed. Greatness that costs nothing is worth nothing. Jesus Himself did not bypass the work. He embraced the cross before the crown. He endured suffering before glory. He showed us that obedience precedes elevation and sacrifice always comes before significance. "No pain, no gain" is not just a saying - it is a spiritual law. If you want a greater calling, expect greater discipline. If you desire deeper faith, expect deeper trials. If you want lasting impact, expect uncomfortable preparation. God is not trying to break you - He is building you into the man He can use to do great and mighty things on the earth. Greatness is not revealed in moments of ease, but in seasons of effort. Put in the work. Stay faithful. Endure the pain.

On the other side of discipline is strength. On the other side of obedience is authority. And on the other side of the process is true greatness. So don't resent what you have to go through to be great. Don't despise the struggle. Don't quit in the tension. The work you're putting in today is preparing you for the weight of tomorrow's responsibility. Every unseen effort, every disciplined choice, every moment of perseverance is strengthening you for what lies ahead. Tomorrow's responsibilities will carry weight, and only those who have trained their character and faith today will be able to bear it without breaking. God never places great responsibility on an unprepared soul. He shapes you in the quiet, in the struggle, and in the process. Stay faithful in the work now, because what you are becoming today is what will sustain you when more is entrusted to you tomorrow. What must you do to be a great man of God? Thankfully, the Bible has a lot to say about what it means to be a real man.

1 Cor. 16:13,14 (ESV) says, "Be watchful, stand firm in the faith, act like men, be strong. Let all you do be done in love." Having bulging muscles and the ability to hunt with a bow and arrow makes you awesome, it doesn't make you a man. To be a real man you must be watchful, alert, awake. You must stand firmly committed to the faith. A real man does not drift with the crowd or bend under pressure. He stands on unyielding convictions, rooted in truth and guided by what is right even when it costs him something. His courage is not loud or reckless; it is steady, disciplined, and proven by action when fear would tell him to retreat. He chooses to do what must be done, not what feels easy. True strength is not measured by domination but by responsibility. A real man grows strong in character, faith, and resolve and he uses that strength to strengthen others. He lifts his brothers when they are weary, sharpens them when they are dull, and stands shoulder to shoulder with them in the fight.

A real man is not defined by how loud he speaks when life is easy, but by how firmly he stands when life turns hostile. Prov. 24:10 says, "If you faint in the day of adversity, your strength is small." Adversity is the proving ground of manhood. Every man will face hardship, resistance, disappointment, and spiritual warfare. The difference between a weak man and a strong man is not the absence of trouble, but the presence of resolve. A real man understands that adversity is not sent to destroy him, but to reveal what is in him. Pressure does not create character - it exposes it. When the battle comes, excuses fall away. Complaints are silenced. What remains is faith, courage, and conviction. Strong men do not run away, they do not faint, grow weary, or collapse in the corner. On the day of battle, a real man's strength is great not because he trusts his own power, but because he has learned to lean fully on God, whose strength never fails. He knows that strength is forged long before the fight ever begins.

A man of strength does not retreat at resistance. He does not collapse under pressure. He does not surrender when the fight gets uncomfortable. Instead, he rises. He presses forward. He holds his ground. Why? Because he knows that God has entrusted him with responsibility over his life, his family, his calling, and his legacy. The battlefield reveals the difference between men who talk about faith and men who walk by faith. When adversity comes, the real man tightens his grip on God, lifts his eyes higher, and advances anyway. The day of adversity is the day of revelation. It reveals who trained. It reveals who prepared. It reveals who trusted God before the storm ever arrived. And when the battle finally comes, the real man stands strong not because the fight is easy, but because his foundation is solid. His strength is great, because his faith is anchored. He does not faint. He does not quit. He does not back down. He fights. He endures. He overcomes. Because a real man was built for the battle.

Make no apologies for being a man. God did not make a mistake when He formed you with strength, courage, and responsibility. Ex.15:3 declares that the Lord is a warrior mighty in battle, fearless in purpose, unwavering in truth. And you were made in His image. Biblical manhood is not arrogance or brutality; it is strength under control, courage guided by righteousness, and power submitted to God. A man anchored in truth stands firm when others retreat, protects what is entrusted to him, and leads with conviction and humility. He does not shrink back from responsibility, nor does he soften the truth to gain approval. In a world that often pressures men to apologize for their strength, God calls you to own it - to rise up, stand tall, and walk boldly in your calling. Be strong. Be faithful. Be courageous. You were made to reflect the heart of a Warrior King. The challenge is we live in a world that doesn't want men to be men. The more feminine men are, the more accepted they will be in this backslidden culture.

To discover the true purpose of being a man and what manhood is all about, you must go back to the beginning of the Bible. The book of Genesis tells us God spoke and galaxies leapt into existence. At His word, stars ignited, oceans gathered, mountains rose, and time itself began to move. Creation obeyed the sound of His voice. But when it came to you, God did something different. Gen. 2:7 says, "And the Lord God formed man of the dust of the ground, and breathed into his nostrils the breath of life, and the man became a living creature." Do not apologize for the way God has formed you, about the way He created you to be. He spoke into existence the stars and everything else, but He formed you on purpose with His own hands. Scripture tells us that God shaped man from the dust of the ground. He did not shout you into existence - He stooped down. He did not merely command you to be - He crafted you with intention. His hands formed your frame, your mind, your heart, your potential.

Before you ever took a breath, God was already involved - molding, shaping, designing. He formed you with care, breathed life into you, and placed His image within you. You are not mass-produced; you are hand-crafted by the Creator of the universe. The same God who flung stars into space paused long enough to personally form you. That alone tells you your value. Every detail of your creation was deliberate. Nothing about you is accidental. The stars declare God's power; you declare His purpose. God did not merely create you to exist - He created you to express His will on the earth. The stars reveal who God is; your life reveals what God desires. They show His greatness from a distance. You demonstrate His heart up close. Where the stars declare His glory in the heavens, you declare His glory in your home, your work, your relationships, and your daily decisions. You are His voice in a hurting world, His hands in a needy generation, His light in dark places. You are a man of God.

God breathed into this shell of a man His own Spirit and this is when this mound of dirt became a man. Adam opened his eyes and the first man in human history came face-to-face with his Heavenly Father. That's what real men are created for, to have a face-to-face, one-on-one relationship with the living God. Real strength is not found in emotional distance or spiritual indifference. It is found in the courage to draw near to God without masks, titles, or excuses. A real man does not hide behind religion - he pursues relationship. He does not settle for knowing about God - he insists on knowing God personally. Every man who has ever shaken the world for God was first a man who stood alone with Him. God is still calling men out of the noise, out of the crowd, and out of shallow faith into a personal encounter with Him. That's what real men are created for - to know God, to walk with Him, to hear His voice, and to stand face-to-face with the living God. Everything else flows from that place.

It doesn't matter how loud your motorcycle is, how many guns you own, how many tattoos you have, or how many beers you can drink. What matters is does the Spirit of God dwell in you and do you have a one-on-one relationship with Almighty God? If the answer is yes, then you can step up and be the real man God called you to be. Gen. 2:8, "And the Lord God planted a garden in Eden, in the east, and there He put the man whom He had formed." Notice that the man was not created in the garden, he was created in the wilderness. Adam's first breath was not taken in safety - it was taken in open territory. Before Eden was planted, Adam existed in the raw world God Himself had made. This matters. God did not take a timid creature and ask him to survive the wilderness. He formed a wilderness-ready man and then gave him a garden to steward. Jesus fasted in the wilderness. He prayed in lonely places. He faced temptation head-on. And then He said, "Follow Me."

The original man was made wild at heart and so should be all the men in the world today. It's in the wilderness that faith is tested, strength is revealed, identity is forged, and men discover who they really are. God still forms men there and He is still calling men to reclaim what was always theirs. Real men have a wild heart submitted to God and a strong spirit under authority. They are men who stand, guard, build, and lead. When a man loses his wilderness, he loses his edge. When he loses his edge, he loses his identity. This is why real men don't like to sit around a little table and talk about their feelings. No, they want to go hunting, watch a rough and tumble football game, cheer on the crazy bull-riders. They want to watch two fighters beat each other up inside a cage, craving the thrill of a stunning knockout. The enemy doesn't attack the femininity of a woman, but an all-out attack is raging against the masculinity of a man. What should you do? Own your identity! Act like a man!

Next, Gen. 2:15 says, "The Lord God took the man and put him in the Garden of Eden to work it and keep it." The first thing God gave man was work to enjoy. Notice that Adam had a job before he had a wife. Work was not the result of the fall. Before there was sin, there was work. Work was not a punishment. Work was not a curse. Work was a privilege. Sin came later. Sweat came later. Frustration came later. But purpose came first. Men were created to work, and God invites all men to be co-creators with Him. He formed the world, then entrusted it to man's hands to cultivate, protect, build, and expand. Through work, a man reflects the nature of God Himself. When a man works with purpose, diligence, and integrity, he partners with God's design. Work gives direction to his strength, meaning to his effort, and dignity to his life. A man is never more fulfilled than when he is doing the work God placed before him. Work is not just what a man does - it is part of who he was created to be.

God gets Eden started and then tells Adam there is work He wants him to do. Adam wasn't wandering the garden bored or waiting on God to bring him a companion to associate with - he was occupied with his assignment from on high. Men of God need more than a job, they need a calling and a career. Adam's calling was to subdue and cultivate. A job may pay the bills, but a calling gives a man purpose. Men of God were not created merely to punch a clock - they were created to build, lead, protect, and serve with intention. A job can sustain a man's body, but only a calling sustains his spirit. A career shaped by God's calling becomes more than work - it becomes an assignment. When a man understands why he was created, his work gains dignity, direction, and impact. He stops working just to survive and starts laboring to leave a legacy. Men of God don't just need employment. They need a calling to answer, a destiny to fulfill, and a career to steward faithfully.

The second thing God gave Adam was a will to obey. Notice there was only one "thou shall not" in the Garden of Eden. Gen. 2:16,17 says, "You may surely eat of every tree of the garden, but of the tree of the knowledge of good and evil you shall not eat." God did not design you to operate like a machine. Obedience must be voluntary. It must not be forced. There must be no coercion. Forced obedience may produce outward compliance, but it can never shape the heart. God is not seeking robots driven by fear or pressure; He desires willing sons and daughters who choose to obey out of love and trust. True obedience flows from a surrendered will, not manipulation or control. It is a response to truth, not intimidation. Voluntary obedience reveals faith, humility, and genuine devotion because what is freely given is always more meaningful than what is demanded. God invites us to obey, but He never forces us. And when we choose obedience freely, it becomes an act of worship, not obligation.

Real men obey God because they know it's the right thing to do, because they desire to do it, and because they take pleasure in obeying God. When you love and trust God, you do things the way He wants them done. You obey Him completely at all times. In Gen. 12:1 God appeared to Abraham and told him to leave his father's house and go to a land He would show him. Notice vs. 4, "So Abraham went, as the Lord had told him." As a real man, you must value obedience to God above all else. Don't question the outcome of your obedience. Make up your mind that when God speaks you will do what He says with unquestioned obedience. Is. 1:19 says, "If you are willing and obedient, you shall eat the good of the land." Obedience is the key to all success. When you choose to follow God's instructions, even when it is difficult or inconvenient, you invite His power, provision, and protection into your life. Obedience activates faith, releases favor, and brings clarity where confusion once lived.

The third thing God gave Adam was a woman to love. He said, "It is not good that the man should be alone; I will make a helper fit for him" (Gen. 2:18). God then put Adam to sleep and took one of his ribs and closed up its place with flesh. Vs. 22, "And the rib that the Lord had taken from the man He made into a woman and brought her to the man." God's words in Genesis reveal His heart for relationship. From the very beginning, the Lord declared that isolation was not His design for humanity. Man was created strong, purposeful, and called but was incomplete alone. God's solution was not merely companionship, but a helper fit for him - one who complements, strengthens, and walks alongside in shared purpose. This verse reminds us that we were never meant to journey through life in solitude. God works through godly relationships to sharpen us, support us, and reflect His love. True strength is not found in standing alone, but in standing together united in purpose and empowered by His design.

Notice that Adam had everything in order in his life before God gave him a wife to love. You've got to have a job, be willing to obey, and get your life in order before you can be trusted with one of God's precious daughters. God does not attach a woman to a man who has nowhere to go and nothing to do. Purpose precedes partnership. This is why Eve was introduced after Adam was positioned, prepared, and productive. Adam walked with God before he ever walked with Eve. God spoke directly to Adam. He gave him instruction, identity, and boundaries before marriage existed. Adam learned God's voice, God's presence, and God's authority first. Marriage was never meant to introduce a man to God -

it was meant to join two people who already know Him. Eve was not given to give Adam purpose - she was given to come alongside the purpose he already had. Eve was not sent to rescue Adam from dysfunction. She was formed to enhance a life that was already ordered.

| 3 |

"TAKE CHARGE"

God has given every man a mantle to carry. That mantle is to be a man of God in a sinful world. All men today need to act like men. You become a man by acting like a man. Manhood is not something that arrives with age - it is forged through action. A boy may grow older, but a man grows stronger by choosing responsibility, discipline, and purpose. You do not become a man by waiting to feel ready; you become a man by stepping up when it is time to stand. A man is revealed by what he does when no one is watching. He keeps his word when it costs him. He works when it would be easier to quit. He tells the truth when a lie would protect his image. Strength is not proven by talk, posture, or appearance, but by consistent, righteous action. Manhood requires courage to lead, to serve, to protect, and to endure. A man does not run from difficulty; he takes charge and faces it head-on. He understands that pressure is not meant to crush him but to shape him into the man he is supposed to be.

Like iron sharpened by iron, character is formed through resistance. A man does not allow emotions, appetites, or impulses to rule him. He governs himself so he can be trusted with greater responsibility. True strength is not loud or reckless; it is steady, dependable, and controlled. You become a man by doing what must be done, not what feels good in the moment. By showing up when others withdraw. By carrying weight instead of avoiding it. By building rather than tearing down. By serving something greater than yourself. Manhood is not a title given - it is a calling to be answered. And every day, with every choice, you decide whether you will answer that call. Like never before, God needs men to act like men. Every day He wants you to step up and do what men are supposed to do. Before David died he charged his son Solomon, saying, "So be strong, act like a man" (1 Kings 2:2). Other translations say, "Prove yourself a man." David is saying you can be a man and not act like a man.

It's not enough to be something, you must act it out. You must act out what you are. God never separates who you are from how you live. In His design, identity always produces action. A tree is known by its fruit - not its roots. Roots matter, but fruit is the evidence that life is present. Spiritual maturity is not measured by how much you know, but by how faithfully you walk out what you know. Your actions preach louder than your words. Your walk speaks before your mouth ever opens. The world is not persuaded by what you believe - it is persuaded by how you live. The problem in the world today is a complete lack of masculinity in its men. There is a masculine dignity that God has placed within you that is quiet, powerful, and unshakable and you must call it out for all the world to see. This dignity is not to be hidden, diluted, or apologized for. It is not arrogance, noise, or domination; it is strength under control, courage rooted in conviction, and responsibility embraced without complaint.

Everything spiritual is about authority. God has established three institutions of authority for mankind. He established government (Rom. 13), the church (Eph. 4), and the family (Eph. 5). God then made Jesus the King over these institutions. When Jesus is not King over a nation's government, authority loses its moral anchor, justice becomes distorted, and chaos inevitably fills the vacuum left by the absence of righteous leadership. If Jesus is not acknowledged as King of the Church, human opinions replace divine authority and truth is slowly compromised, and all authority is lost. Where Christ does not reign, a falling away is the inevitable outcome. Such a path always ends in apostasy, a falling away from the truth, spiritual treason and desertion. If Jesus is not King of the family, everyone competes for control, and selfish desires begin to clash. Without His authority guiding hearts, unity fades and tension grows. Where Christ is not enthroned, hostility inevitably fills the void He was meant to occupy.

Authority is required to fulfill your role of masculinity, and it all begins in the home. Eph. 5:23,24 say, "For the husband is the head of the wife, as Christ is the head of the church. Therefore, just as the church is subject to Christ, so let the wives be to their own husbands in everything." As the head of your home, leadership is more than a title - it is a calling. God has entrusted you with the responsibility to cover your family spiritually, care for them emotionally, and provide for them physically. Your walk with God sets the tone for the household. Your words shape the atmosphere. Your actions model faith, love, discipline, and integrity. To lead well means you pray first, listen closely, and act selflessly. It means standing firm in truth, showing compassion in weakness, and taking responsibility even when it's hard. When you lead with humility, courage, and love, you create a home where faith grows, hearts are secure, and lives are strengthened. Know that your wife and children are the fruit of your leadership.

Christian men in the world today need to get their act together because as goes the man, so goes the family, the community, and the world. It all starts with you. Christian men who act like men are the ones who make the difference in this crazy, mixed-up, upside-down world. We need to rise up and lead the way, and it all starts with you leading your family and doing what God has called you to do. The world doesn't need weaker men - it needs men who will lead like men, the way God designed them to lead. God created men to stand, not shrink; to protect, not retreat; to take responsibility, not pass blame. Real leadership isn't about domination or ego - it's about strength under control, conviction anchored in truth, and courage that serves others. When men lead the way God intended, families are steadied, communities are strengthened, and chaos loses ground. The world is desperate for men who will rise with integrity, lead with humility, and act with bold obedience.

Now is the time to reject passivity, silence, and compromise, and to step fully into the calling God placed on your life. Live like a man of God and lead like a man. God is speaking clearly to men in this generation saying it's time to grow up and put away spiritual immaturity, excuses, and half-hearted living. He is calling men to take responsibility, to lead with integrity, and to live out their faith with strength, discipline, and obedience. The days of drifting are over. Now is the moment to stand firm, walk boldly, and become the men He created you to be. Now is the time to make your walk with Jesus the top priority of your life on a daily basis. Stop messing around. Take up your cross and actually proclaim Jesus to your family and the world you live in. Act like a man. Lead your family and proclaim the gospel message to your lost loved ones, your neighbors, and your co-workers. You are not ashamed of the gospel so be actively involved in the building up of the kingdom of God wherever you go.

Husbands and wives are equally valuable in God's eyes. However, they are not equal in their roles, traits, and strengths. God has assigned husbands to be the leader of his wife and home. Godly wives want their husbands to lead and take charge. Foolish wives want the role of leader. They quote Eph. 5:21, "Submit to one another out of reverence for Christ." They say, "We're partners. Everything is fifty-fifty." This verse is often misunderstood. It's totally about the posture of the heart. Each are supposed to do what's best for the other. You submit to one another by fulfilling your God-given roles. The way the wife submits to her husband is to do as the church submits to Christ. The way the husband submits to his wife is by submitting to Christ and leading his wife as Christ leads the church. The husband and wife are not co-leaders in the home. It's been said that anything with two heads is a monster. The bottom line is the husband is the leader, and the wife is the follower. Period. That's how God set it up.

God establishes order in the home, calling husbands to lead with love and wives to respond with willing submission to that godly leadership. It is not taken lightly when a wife knowingly resists or rejects righteous leadership that aligns with God's Word. The Bible equates rebellion against God-ordained authority with serious spiritual consequences. 1 Sam. 15:23 declares, "For rebellion is as the sin of witchcraft." This reveals that rebellion is not merely a relational issue but is in fact a spiritual matter. Just as witchcraft seeks control apart from God, rebellion rejects God's design and invites disorder. God does not call wives to submit to abuse or sin, but He does call them to honor and support righteous leadership by respecting, encouraging, and standing faithfully beside their husbands as partners in God's purpose, helping them lead with humility, courage, and integrity. When submission is replaced with resistance, the home suffers, unity is fractured, and spiritual authority is undermined.

True freedom, peace, and blessing flow when God's order is honored and His Word is obeyed. Husbands are blessed when they submit to God, wives are blessed when they submit to their husbands. God doesn't make you submit to Him, and neither should you force your wife to submit to you. The way you teach your wife to submit to your authority is by way of example. Show her by example what submission looks like. You model it for her; you don't demand it from her. Let her see you submitting to God's Word and the laws of the land. Be a spiritual man and a noble citizen. Let her see you submitting to the leadership at your local church. Heb. 13:17, "Obey your spiritual leaders and do as they say." When you rebel against those in authority over you, you're training your wife and children to rebel against you and your authority. Remember, what you sow is what you will reap. If you show honor to those over you, you will be honored by those under you.

Masculine men take responsibility for their wife and children. They do not shift blame, make excuses, or abandon their post when life gets hard. A real man understands that his wife and children are not burdens to escape but sacred responsibilities to steward. He stands as protector, provider, and guide - emotionally, spiritually, and practically. A God-fearing man leads with love, choosing compassion, patience, and humility as reflections of Christ in his daily walk. He leads with strength, standing firm on truth, protecting what God has entrusted to him, and refusing to compromise his convictions. When love guides his heart and strength anchors his actions, his leadership brings peace, order, and blessing to everyone within his influence. He shows up when it's inconvenient, speaks truth with compassion, and makes hard decisions for the good of his family. He works diligently, prays faithfully, and models integrity so his children have a living example of character to follow.

A man's true masculinity takes ownership of his words, his actions, and his calling to cover his household with wisdom, courage, and unwavering commitment. You may not be personally guilty for what your loved ones do wrong, but you are responsible for their actions. If your wife abuses the use of credit cards, you're not guilty for what she did wrong but you are responsible to pay for it. If your teenager smashes the family car, it is your responsibility to step in and fix the problem. You may not have made the mess your family is in, but you are responsible to clean it up. Sad to say, men have been shunning their responsibility as men since time began. Adam blamed Eve for eating the forbidden fruit instead of taking responsibility for what she did. He even blamed God for giving Eve to him in the first place. He "passed the buck" without taking responsibility as the leader of the home. Don't "pass the buck" of responsibility to the people you're responsible to lead. You take the responsibility.

Over time, your leadership sets the direction and atmosphere of your home, shaping whether your family grows strong or slowly drifts off course. The choices you make, the example you live, and the values you consistently model will either build stability and confidence or invite confusion and weakness. Faithful, intentional leadership creates a foundation where your family can flourish, even through life's challenges. Just remember, if your family has a problem, it is your responsibility to fix it. Follow the example of Jesus. Rom. 5:8 says, "While we were yet sinners, Christ died for us." He never sinned but took on the responsibility to pay off the debt of our sin. When a man leads with godly authority that is marked by love, humility, and responsibility - he creates an atmosphere of trust and safety. In that environment, a wife's godly response is willing, respectful obedience that flows from partnership and shared purpose, not compulsion. She'll follow your lead and obey your leadership.

Many women, however, don't submit because of fear. They're afraid their husband will let them down. This fear is what causes wives to try to control their husbands. A wife's attempt to take charge often flows from fear of being hurt, abandoned, or losing security rather than coming from a desire for power. That is part of the curse of the fall of man. God told Eve, "Your husband will rule over you and you'll try to control him" (Gen. 3:16). Controlling women are fearful women. Control often grows out of fear - fear of loss, uncertainty, or being vulnerable. When a woman tries to control everything around her, it is often a sign that she is seeking safety where trust and confidence have been wounded. They fear they won't be led properly so they try to take control themselves. These wives need to know there is safety and blessing in submission to godly authority. Being under your leadership will give them a sense of safety and peace. They know they don't have to figure everything out. All they have to do is trust you as you trust God.

Jesus gave Himself for the Church, laying down His life in perfect love so that His people might be redeemed, protected, and made whole. In the same way, godly leaders are called to lead by example, sacrificing comfort, recognition, and personal gain for the good of those entrusted to their care. True leadership mirrors the cross - serving first, loving deeply, and giving all so others may flourish. A pastor sacrifices for his church by pouring out his life in prayer, service, and leadership, often carrying burdens few ever see. A husband sacrifices for his wife by loving her selflessly, placing her needs above his own, and leading with strength, humility, and faithfulness. Parents sacrifice for their children by giving their time, energy, comfort, and dreams so the next generation can grow, thrive, and walk in purpose.1 John 3:16 (TPT) says, "This is how we have discovered love's reality: Jesus sacrificed His life for us. Because of this great love, we should be willing to lay down our lives for one another,"

The majority of all divorces are initiated by women because their husbands haven't made the sacrifices they are required to make. Real men sacrifice for women and children. When the Titanic sank, it was the women and children who got on the lifeboats first. The women and children got set free while the men went down with the ship. That's the way it should be. A man sacrifices and works two jobs if necessary so his wife can stay home and take care of their children. It is a godly and noble thing for a man to do whatever is best for his wife and children, even when it requires sacrifice and self-denial. True strength is shown not in selfish ambition, but in laying down personal desires to protect, provide for, and nurture the family God has entrusted to him. When a man lives this way, he reflects the heart of Christ and builds a legacy of love, security, and faith for generations to come. In return, the proper response from his wife is gratitude. Every man knows that the blessings of a grateful wife are beyond measure.

Masculinity takes the initiative. It does not wait to be told what needs to be done. Real men understand they have been given both the power and the responsibility to act, stepping forward when others hesitate. They lead by example, making decisions with courage rather than excuses. True masculinity takes charge first, knowing that action sets the direction for everyone who follows. Initiative is the opposite of passivity - it is the willingness to lead, act, and take responsibility rather than waiting to be pushed. It is not right or proper for wives to drag their husbands to church; men are called to step forward on their own and lead themselves and their families spiritually. Real men take the initiative to take their family to church and to have home Bible studies. A real man takes charge by taking the initiative to plan good things on purpose for his wife and children. When a man leads with vision, thoughtfulness, and action, his wife feels secure and his children grow confident, knowing someone is intentionally guiding their future.

Jesus took the initiative. Rom. 5:8 says, "While we were yet sinners, Christ died for us." Jesus made the first move, and we are called to do the same. He said in Matt. 28:20 that we should "obey everything I have commanded you." Boldly take the lead and obey all that God has instructed you to do. Jesus said in John 14:15, "If you love Me, keep My commandments." Take the initiative to obey God without delay, trusting that His commands are given for your good and His glory. True faith is not passive - it moves first, acts boldly, and follows God even when the path is unclear. When you do everything God commands, you position yourself to experience His power, favor, and purpose at work in your life. Lead by example. Rise up and take action. If God tells you to do something, do it with all your heart and soul and strength. Don't be forced to obey. Take the initiative and do it willingly. What you sow is what you'll reap. The way you respond to God will be the way your wife and children will respond to you.

| 4 |

"TOUGH AND TENDER"

The world today is desperate for solutions. Nations debate policies. Governments expand programs. Leaders promise reform. Yet despite new laws, new leaders, and new systems, the same problems remain - violence, corruption, broken families, injustice, and moral confusion. The truth be told, the solution to the problems in the world today is not better government but better men. Government can restrain evil, but it cannot transform hearts. Laws can punish wrongdoing, but they cannot produce righteousness. Policies may manage behavior, but they cannot change character. The condition of the world is not primarily a political problem - it is a moral and spiritual problem. Every broken system is ultimately sustained by broken people. Corrupt governments are not created in a vacuum; they are built by corrupt men. Violent societies are not caused by a lack of laws but by a lack of self-control. Collapsing families are not the result of insufficient programs but absent, passive, or irresponsible men.

Prov. 29:2 says, "When the righteous are in authority, the people rejoice; but when the wicked rule, the people groan." The quality of leadership in a nation reflects the quality of the men within it. When men abandon truth, discipline, and responsibility, society pays the price. God's pattern for fixing societal problems has always been to use men who were committed to doing His will. One faithful man named Noah preserved humanity. One obedient man named Abraham birthed a nation. One courageous shepherd named David changed Israel's destiny. One righteous man named Joseph preserved entire civilizations. God's strategy has never been mass legislation - it has always been transformed men who lead with integrity, courage, and humility. No government can teach a man to love his wife, protect his children, tell the truth, work diligently, or walk humbly with God. These virtues are not produced by policy; they are formed through conviction, discipline, and submission to God.

When men reject responsibility, government grows larger to fill the void. But when men stand up - serving, sacrificing, leading, and living righteously - families strengthen, communities stabilize, and societies flourish. The question is not, "What should the government do?" The question is, "What kind of man am I becoming?" Real change begins when men fear God more than public opinion, take responsibility instead of making excuses, lead their homes instead of abandoning them, stand for truth instead of remaining silent, and serve others instead of demanding entitlement. The world does not need louder protests or bigger platforms - it needs men of character, conviction, and courage. If you want a better nation, build better men. If you want justice, raise righteous men. If you want peace, cultivate disciplined men. If you want lasting change, start in the heart. Government can regulate behavior but only God can remake a man. And when men are changed by God, the world changes with them.

The answer to today's global challenges lies not in improved government, but in improved character among men. Unfortunately, in today's world, men are in a weaker position than they've ever been. Why is that? Because our culture has found a way to reduce and diminish masculinity in its men. Look around you and you'll see the literal, biological, emotional, psychological, and spiritual deterioration of masculinity unfolding in real time. Strength has been redefined as passivity, responsibility traded for comfort, and conviction replaced with compromise. Most countries are not in a position of strength because their men don't act like men. If under attack they would have drag queens throw sprinkled cupcakes at the invaders hoping for the right outcome. We live in a world that increasingly creates weak men and unless something changes, there won't be any real men left. The strength, conviction, and backbone required of real men will fade leaving society without leaders willing to stand and protect.

A real man is the man who wants to be like Jesus, the greatest man in the history of the world. No one ever lived with more authority, more courage, more compassion, or more purpose than Him. He did not conquer nations with armies, yet He changed the course of history forever. He did not rule with intimidation, yet demons trembled at His voice. He did not seek applause, yet heaven declared Him the Son of God. He stood firm when others compromised. He spoke truth when it cost Him popularity. He faced suffering without quitting, rejection without bitterness, and death without fear. He laid His life down not because He was weak, but because He was strong enough to love sacrificially. Jesus loved deeply, forgave freely, served humbly, and stood courageously against evil. He stood up for and protected the weak, confronted hypocrisy, and refused to bow to pressure. He was gentle with the broken and fierce against sin. He was disciplined, focused, and unshakably committed to the will of the Father.

What's it like to be like Jesus? He is called the Lion of the tribe of Judah (Rev. 5:5) to display His absolute authority and power over all creation. He is also called the Lamb of God (John 1:16) to illustrate His gentleness and willingness to be the sacrifice for our sins. Real men are both tough and tender. They're a lion for their family and a lamb with their family. 1 Cor. 16:13 tells men to stand firm, be strong, act like men. That's the lion. A real man is a lion when it comes to protection. He stands between danger and his home. He confronts physical, spiritual, emotional, and moral threats without flinching. He refuses passivity. He refuses to be silent. He refuses to retreat when his family needs covering. A lion does not apologize for his strength. He does not explain why he guards what is precious. He roars when the enemy comes near. A real man fights battles his family may never even know existed. He bears pressure so they can rest. He absorbs stress so they can feel secure. This is strength with purpose.

1 Cor. 16:14 says to let everything you do be done in love. That's the lamb. His strength does not make him harsh. His authority does not make him cold. His leadership does not make him distant. With his family, he is patient. He listens to them and comforts them when they are hurting. He stoops low enough to be gentle. A real man knows when to lower his voice, soften his touch, and open his heart. He knows that his family does not need his roar - they need his presence. This is tenderness with intention. Your family wants you to be tender as a lamb when you're with them. Women should feel safe around you just like the woman caught in adultery felt safe around Jesus. Children also loved Jesus and felt safe around Him. Everywhere He went the children were following Him. At the same time, your loved ones need to know that, if needed, a lion will be there to protect them. As a man you are far more important than you think, far more needed than you think, far more powerful than you think.

Jesus Christ is what a real man looks like. Like Him, a real man knows when to be tough, and when to be tender and gracious with those God has called him to care for. A real man knows that strength is not proven by hardness alone, but by discernment. He stands firm and unyielding when truth, righteousness, and protection are required. Yet with those God has entrusted to his care, he leads with a gentle heart, patient hands, and gracious words. True masculinity is the wisdom to balance courage with compassion, reflecting both the power and the kindness of God. If you're only a lion, strength without restraint turns into cruelty, and the ones you're called to protect suffer most. If you're only a lamb, gentleness without courage becomes passivity, and evil goes unchecked in your home. God never called a man to choose between power and compassion, but to carry both with wisdom. A real man is strong enough to confront evil and tender enough to love well, guarding his family with courage and grace.

Men become like the Jesus they behold because what a man believes about Christ ultimately shapes his character, courage, and conduct. If Jesus is seen as weak or passive, men will drift toward softness and compromise; but if He is known as strong, obedient, sacrificial, and bold, men rise to reflect that same strength and resolve. To follow Him rightly, men must know not a distorted image, but the true Man Jesus was - holy, courageous, compassionate, disciplined, and unyielding in obedience to the Father. Jesus is the Lion of Judah and He is tough. He is mighty, fearless, and unyielding in strength. He is a warrior who does not shrink back but stands as the ultimate victor. He rules over His people with righteous authority, guarding them with power and unwavering love. And as a conquering King, He crushes His enemies beneath His feet, proving that no force of darkness can withstand His reign. His kingdom is an eternal kingdom, and He is one to be feared. One day all people will bow down to Him.

Jesus is the Lion, the conquering, victorious King who has triumphed over sin, death, and every power of darkness. A lion conquers because he was created with strength, courage, and authority to rule his domain. He does not survive by hiding or retreating, but by advancing with confidence and purpose. Dominion belongs to those who conquer and that is why the lion is called the king of the beasts and the king of the jungle. A lion represents unmatched strength, predatory ferocity, majesty, and leadership in the natural world. It moves with fearless confidence, ruling its territory with authority and commanding respect by its presence alone. As the king of beasts, the lion symbolizes the courage to lead, the power to protect, and the dominance to prevail. The lion stands as the enduring symbol of a ruler and a king, embodying authority, dominance, and royal dignity. Its fierce power and commanding presence reflect a leadership that inspires both awe and respect, ruling not by weakness but by strength and courage.

Lions are legendary for their strength, beauty, and fearlessness for they were created with a commanding presence that cannot be ignored. No one casually confronts a lion, because its authority is evident before it ever roars. In the same way, God calls His people to walk with quiet confidence, spiritual strength, and unwavering courage, knowing who they are and whose they are. Like a lion, you are bold and confident. You overwhelmingly conquer all your adversaries. You are strong and mighty because greater is He who is in you than he who is in the world. Like a lion, you were not created to live timidly, shrinking back in fear or hesitation. You were designed with boldness woven into your spirit, confidence planted deep within your soul, and courage meant to rise when challenges roar the loudest. The lion does not ask permission to stand strong because it knows who it is. In the same way, when you understand who you are and whose you are, fear loses its voice and intimidation loses its power.

A lion does not panic when opposition appears. It does not retreat at the sound of resistance. Instead, it lifts its head, fixes its gaze, and advances with unshakable confidence. That same strength lives inside you. When adversity comes against you, it is not a signal to withdraw - it is a summons to rise. You are equipped to face opposition head-on, not because the battle is easy, but because you are built for victory. Lions do not survive by luck; they overcome by authority. They walk with a quiet assurance that sends a message before a fight ever begins. In your life, that same authority is released when you stand firm in truth, faith, and purpose. Your confidence does not come from pride - it comes from knowing that you are empowered, strengthened, and upheld beyond your own ability. When you walk forward with bold confidence and unwavering confidence, obstacles that once held you back begin to loosen their grip and lose their power. Your adversaries start shaking by the strength of your resolve.

The lion overwhelms its enemies not by frantic effort, but by decisive action. It knows when to wait and when to strike. Likewise, you are learning to move with wisdom, timing, and clarity. You do not waste energy on fear or doubt. You conserve your strength for the moment it matters most. And when that moment comes, you advance with force, conviction, and resolve. Every adversary you face - whether fear, discouragement, temptation, or opposition - was never meant to defeat you. They exist to reveal your strength. Like a lion emerging victorious from the hunt, you rise stronger, more confident, and more assured with every battle you overcome. Each victory reinforces what was true all along: you are not weak, you are not powerless, and you are not defeated. Like a lion, you are fearless in the face of opposition, relentless in pursuit of purpose, and overwhelming in victory. And as you move forward, let the roar of faith within you remind every challenge you face that you were born to overcome.

The Bible portrays Jesus as a roaring lion taking vengeance on all His enemies. A lion says, "Back off! You'll never defeat me! AARRGGHH!" Rev. 19:15 says, "And He Himself will rule them with a rod of iron. He Himself treads the winepress of the fierceness and wrath of Almighty God." Hosea 11:10 says, "He will roar like a lion. When He roars, then His sons shall come trembling from the west." A lion's roar can be heard up to five miles away. Lions roar to establish their territory and to communicate their power. A lion's face and his roar represent the boldness and strength of God's character. A lion may be the king of the jungle, but the Lion of Judah is the King of kings and Lord of lords (Rev. 19:16). Jesus showed His emotions. He was indignant, He had anger, zeal, and passion. With anger He confronted religious leaders who wanted people to live under the law instead of grace. As a lion, He made a whip and chased the money-changers out of the temple, pushing over many tables as He did so.

Jesus is a lion, but He is also a tender lamb. He was a man of passion, a man who had feelings and emotions. He is the perfect example of what a real man looks like. Lions are tough but lambs are tender. Male lions are radically independent. Lambs, however, are social creatures who like to hang out together. Lions run to a fight, lambs run from a fight. Lions love a war, but lambs don't like conflict of any kind. Lions eat meat, lambs eat grass. Lambs are fluffy and very lovable. They're homeless, they're pacifists. They never attack anyone. If a young child can't go to sleep, you tell them to count sheep. You don't tell them to count lions. Children will run away from a lion but will run to a lamb. The most common emotion of Jesus was compassion. He was tender and loving like a lamb. He would sit down and invite the young children to hug Him and sit on His lap. He loved and His heart went out to people. He was always filled with compassion reminding us that true love is expressed through selfless care for others.

The Bible tells the story of how Jesus went to the bedside of Jairus' daughter because she was sick (Matt. 9:18-26). He could have healed her from a distance, but He wanted to be in her presence. He went to her, spoke to her, loved her. He cared for her and He healed her. That's the ministry of presence. Be there for your family when they need you and even when they don't. Be present in their lives. You are the spiritual, emotional, and relational thermostat in your home. You being there for your family is a ministry. Being at the dinner table is a ministry. Attending your children's sporting events is a ministry. Going to church together is a ministry. Be a lamb to your loved ones. Be compassionate, tender, kind, gracious, loving. Your presence makes them feel safe. It brings a calm assurance that everything is going to be okay, like a steady shelter in the middle of life's storms. When you are there, your strength, consistency, and love create a safe place where your family can rest, trust, and thrive.

Is Jesus a lion? Yes! Rev. 5:5 says, "Weep no more; behold the Lion of the tribe of Judah, the Root of David, has conquered." Is Jesus a lamb? Yes! Vs. 6 says, "And between the throne and the four living creatures and among the elders I saw a Lamb standing, as though it has been slain." Real men who want to be like Jesus must also be a lion and a lamb. You can't be one or the other, you must be both. If you're only a lion, your children will run from you. This is why many daughters get pregnant and run off with their boyfriends. If you're only a lamb, you'll pray instead of physically confronting those who are abusing your family. The safest place in the world for your wife and children should be in your loving arms. Never should they flinch or step back when you draw near to them. Never make your family afraid of you. Be a lamb and show them love and tenderness and compassion. Guard your family with the strength of a roaring lion and dwell with them in the meekness of a tender and gentle lamb.

Wisdom will tell you when to be a lion and when to be a lamb. Lambs are always passive. Men who are only lambs need to rise up and quickly become a lion. Lambs pray for their loved ones, but they don't intervene when trouble comes knocking at their door. That's what lions do. Remember, Jesus didn't pray for the money-changers. He made a whip and drove them out of the temple. Lambs need to know there are times when they need to fight. There are times when you need to take action and protect your loved ones. It is a wonderful thing to be a lamb with your children. But in today's culture, you need to be a lion to protect them from all evil influences. You need to speak up when something needs to be said. You need to act when something needs to be done. Passivity is sin! Praying when you should be fighting is sin! Sometimes you need to rise up and answer your own prayers. Be the leader your family needs! Be the provider! Be the defender! Be the protector! Rise up and act like a real man of God.

| 5 |

"SLAY THE DRAGON"

Real men act like the Jesus, greatest man in the history of the world. In a culture that often defines manhood by power, dominance, or image, Jesus Christ redefines what it truly means to be a man. Real men don't measure themselves by how loud they are, how feared they are, or how much control they wield. Real men measure themselves by how closely they walk with Christ. Jesus was strong yet gentle. He could calm storms with a word, yet He knelt to wash the feet of His disciples. Real men are not threatened by humility. They understand that true strength bows before God and serves others without seeking applause. Jesus stood firm in truth. He never compromised righteousness to fit the culture of His day. Real men live by conviction, choosing what is right over what is easy. They stand firm on truth even when it costs them popularity, comfort, or acceptance, because integrity matters more than applause. A man of conviction would rather stand alone with honor than blend in by compromise.

Jesus loved sacrificially. He laid down His life for others. Real men protect, provide, and give themselves for their families, their communities, and the calling God has placed on their lives. Love, for a real man, is not passive - it is active, intentional, and costly. Jesus was disciplined. He prayed, fasted, and sought the Father daily. Real men cultivate a private life with God before they attempt to lead publicly. They understand that authority flows from obedience and that spiritual power is forged in quiet places of surrender. Jesus was courageous. He faced opposition, rejection, and the cross without retreating. Real men confront fear with faith, pain with perseverance, and trials with unwavering trust in God. Courage is not the absence of fear - it is obedience in spite of it. Jesus showed compassion without weakness and strength without cruelty. Real men are not hardened by the world; they are refined by God. They speak truth with love, correct with grace, and lead with integrity.

To act like Jesus is not to be soft - it is to be unshakeable. It is to walk in authority without arrogance, humility without insecurity, and power without pride. Real men act like Jesus. And when they do, families are strengthened, communities are transformed, and the world sees a living picture of God's love in action. It is so significant that you be a man who is both tough and tender like Jesus was (Rev. 5:5,6). It all starts with having strength and masculinity. Why? Because today we live in a world that rewards comfort, excuses, and convenience and, in doing so, it quietly produces weak men. Strength is no longer forged through discipline, sacrifice, and responsibility, but eroded by endless distractions, shallow pleasures, and the avoidance of hardship. God never called men to be soft or passive; He called them to be strong in character, anchored in truth, and unashamed to stand when others shrink back. A man of God stands firm, serves sacrificially, and follows Christ even when the path demands everything he has.

Since the fall of man in the Garden of Eden, all of human history has been a relentless war between good and evil. From that first act of disobedience, darkness has sought to corrupt what God created for good, while truth and righteousness have continually called mankind back to Him. Every generation stands on this same battlefield, choosing whether to align with the purposes of God or the deception of the enemy. Everything fell apart when the dragon slithered into the garden, and our father Adam chose silence instead of resistance. Evil advanced not because it was unstoppable, but because the one entrusted to guard what was holy did not fight back. From that moment on, history became a battlefield, calling every man to stand where Adam fell. Unless something drastically changes, there won't be any real men left in the not-too-distant future. If men do not rise to reclaim discipline, conviction, and purpose, the next generation will inherit weakness disguised as progress.

Evil does not stop itself. It never has. It never will. It never pauses to consider the damage it causes. It does not grow tired. It does not retreat because people hope it will. Evil advances whenever it is allowed to move unchecked. History proves this over and over again - darkness grows strongest where good men grow silent. This is why every generation faces a moment of reckoning. Not because evil suddenly appears, but because men must decide whether they will confront it or coexist with it. Real men need to step up and stop the evil that is in the world. We need to slay the dragon. One of the most dangerous lies in modern Christianity is the idea that goodness is passive. Somewhere along the way, many men were taught that being Christlike means avoiding conflict, never raising their voice, and staying out of the fight altogether. Evil moves the moment resistance weakens or disappears. When good men stay silent and refuse to stand, darkness fills the vacuum they leave behind.

The dragon looks different in every era, but its nature never changes. The dragon thrives on fear. It feeds on silence. It grows when men convince themselves someone else will deal with it. But scripture makes one thing clear: God never intended for men to be spectators in the battle between light and darkness. From the beginning, men were created to guard and protect what God entrusted to them. When Adam failed to confront the serpent, the cost was catastrophic. Silence in the presence of evil is never neutral; it is destructive. Real men understand that strength is not about dominance - it is about responsibility. A real man stands not because it is easy, but because it is necessary. He stands when truth is under attack. He stands when the innocent are threatened. He stands when lies become normalized and righteousness becomes mocked. Courage does not mean living without fear. It means choosing to act because purpose, conviction, and your calling matters more than the fear you feel.

God is still looking for men who will stand in the gap - men who will refuse to let darkness pass unchallenged into their homes, their communities, or their culture. These men are not driven by applause or recognition; they are anchored by purpose and conviction. They serve faithfully and quietly, content to let their character and obedience speak louder than any spotlight. They are steady, grounded, and unmovable because they know who they serve. Most dragons are not slain on public stages. They are slain in private decisions: When a man chooses integrity over convenience. When he confronts sin instead of excusing it. When he protects his family instead of prioritizing comfort. When he speaks truth instead of remaining silent to keep peace. Slaying the dragon often looks like consistency, discipline, and courage in ordinary moments. It looks like saying "no" when compromise is easier. It looks like standing alone when others bow. It looks like obedience when disobedience is applauded.

The enemy loses power every time a man refuses to yield ground. War is in the DNA of every man, and this is the hour for men to rise - not with arrogance, but with authority. Not with violence, but with backbone. Not with compromise, but with conviction. God is not looking for perfect men. He is looking for available men, men who will say, "Here I am. Send me" (Is. 6:8). The dragon will not slay itself and the future belongs to the men who decide to stand up, take responsibility, and slay the dragon. Evil will continue to advance wherever God's men remain silent, passive, or unwilling to act. Darkness is not defeated by good intentions, but by righteous men who are willing to stand, speak, and intervene. When God's men step up with courage, conviction, and obedience, evil loses its ground and light takes its place. Real men of God carry a deep desire for strength and masculinity, not as a display of ego, but as a calling to be capable, disciplined, and prepared. They want conflict, struggle, effort, success.

The truth be told, every godly man, in some shape or form, possesses a capacity for violence. This truth may sound unsettling at first, but it is neither ungodly nor accidental. It is designed. What defines a godly man is not the absence of strength, but the mastery of it. God never intended men to be weak. He created men with strength, resolve, and the ability to confront threats - physical, spiritual, and moral. Scripture repeatedly portrays righteous men as warriors, protectors, builders, and defenders. The danger is not strength itself; the danger is strength without restraint or strength without righteousness. A man who lacks the capacity for violence is not necessarily godly - he may simply be harmless. But a man who has strength and chooses discipline, restraint, and obedience to God is walking in biblical maturity. True godliness does not erase a man's edge; it sanctifies it. The capacity for violence, when submitted to God, becomes courage. It becomes the willingness to stand when others shrink back.

A godly man does not look for fights, but neither does he flee from them when righteousness demands action. He understands that meekness is the disciplined channeling of strength for God's purposes rather than self-serving ends. The modern world often tries to teach men to suppress their strength rather than submit it to God. But scripture calls men higher. A godly man is not passive. He is dangerous when he is going in the right direction. He is dangerous to darkness and anything that threatens what God has entrusted to him. The goal is not to become violent men, but capable men who know they have strength, who have faced it honestly, and who have placed it under the lordship of Christ. When strength is sanctified, it no longer destroys; it defends, builds, and preserves. A godly man is not harmless. A godly man sets himself apart in holiness, trains himself in discipline, and remains ready for action. And that readiness - when governed by love - is exactly what the world desperately needs.

Retired Lieutenant Colonel David Grossman conducts seminars on the psychology of lethal force. in his book "On Combat" he talks about sheep, wolves, and sheepdogs. He says a person with no capacity for violence is a sheep. A person who has capacity for violence but has no love is a wolf. A person who has a capacity for violence but has love for his fellow man is a sheepdog. He is a warrior who is walking the hero's path. A sheepdog is a protector, one who steps in to help the helpless and those who are mistreated. Men who are sheepdogs watch out for people who are at risk, people who are being abused and oppressed. A godly man uses his strength not for dominance but for defense, stepping forward when others step back. He refuses to ignore injustice, choosing instead to shield the helpless and confront wrongdoing with courage and compassion. In doing so, he reflects the heart of God by becoming a safe place for the vulnerable and a voice for those who cannot speak for themselves.

Masculinity is a mindset. It is not revealed in muscle, volume, or outward dominance. It is revealed in the way a man thinks, chooses, endures, and leads when no one is watching. True masculinity begins on the inside and expresses itself outwardly through conviction, responsibility, and moral courage. A masculine mindset understands that strength is stewardship. A man does not use his strength to control others, but to carry weight for his family, his community, and his calling. He accepts responsibility instead of avoiding it. He does not wait to be forced into maturity; he chooses it. This is the mindset that says, "If it matters, I will own it." True masculinity is rooted in discipline rather than indulgence. It recognizes that freedom is not found in doing whatever feels good, but in mastering oneself. A man with this mindset governs his emotions, restrains his impulses, and aligns his actions with truth rather than convenience. He understands that self-control is not weakness - it is power properly directed.

A masculine mindset embraces courage with clarity. It does not mean recklessness or aggression; it means standing firm when retreat would be easier. It is the courage to speak truth, to protect what is right, and to endure hardship without abandoning integrity. This kind of courage does not need applause for it is anchored in purpose. Masculinity is also a mindset of service, not entitlement. He leads by example, not by demand. He understands that leadership is proven by sacrifice, consistency, and faithfulness over time. Masculinity is a mindset rooted in identity and conviction. A man who knows who he is does not need to perform for approval or shrink in the face of opposition. He is steady, grounded, and resilient. He is anchored and unwavering, sustained by strength that comes from within. He knows that masculinity is not something to prove - it is something to live out every day. When a man's mindset is aligned with truth, strength, and responsibility, his life will reflect it in every area he touches.

You can't just call yourself a man, you have to act like a man based on having the right mindset. Real men possess the strength of will to stand behind their words, not merely speak them. Their character is proven when resolve turns conviction into consistent action, even when it costs them something. They don't just talk the talk; they walk the walk. Ex. 2:17-20 tells the story of the daughters of a priest in Egypt who went to water their father's flock. As they did this, some bully shepherds came and drove them away. Watch what happens next. Vs. 17 says, "But Moses stood up and helped them, and watered their flock." Moses was a stranger to these women, but he helped them anyway. That was a "man move" Moses made. This was a masculine act. He didn't choose self-preservation but chose intervention. This story shows us that God put us here to make a difference in the world we live in. Sometimes that means to stand up for people who are helpless and can't protect themselves.

God has already placed within you the strength and confidence needed to slay the dragon standing before you. The victory you walk in is not merely for your own deliverance, but as a testimony and shield for others who are now coming under attack from the enemy. As you stand firm in faith, your courage becomes an intervention point where fear is broken, hope is restored, and others are empowered to overcome. Moses stood up for the women watering their father's flock and David stepped up when Goliath oppressed the army of Israel. Jesus stepped up and saved us when we couldn't save ourselves. He intervened on our behalf. When you choose to come to someone's rescue, God positions you as a living answer to their prayers for help and deliverance. What they have cried out to heaven for, He often sends through willing hands, courageous hearts, and obedient footsteps. In stepping forward, you become the instrument through which God turns desperation into hope and bondage into freedom.

Always be ready to stand up for the widow, the fatherless, and the single mother who is struggling to make ends meet because compassion in action reflects the heart of God. When you step in to help carry their burden, you become a living answer to prayers spoken in silence and tears. Stand up for those who are being bullied by others, for the wife who has been physically abused by her husband. Staying silent and doing nothing only strengthens the oppressor, but courage gives the wounded a voice and a path to safety. Help the elderly with practical acts of kindness, things like mowing their lawns, changing the oil in their cars, and handling the tasks that have become difficult for them. By serving in these simple yet meaningful ways, you honor their dignity and live out compassion through action, not just words. Help the homeless and those stranded in a broken car on the highway. Encourage one another. Speak life to those who are hurting. Build each other up. Put wind in their sail.

When God completed creation, He declared it good. Gut when He formed man in His own image, He called it was "very good," marking humanity as the crown of His work (Gen. 1:31). This declaration reminds us that our value, purpose, and dignity come directly from God, not from performance, comparison, or circumstance. It is very good to be a man created by God with purpose, strength, and responsibility. A man who is strong, confident, and ambitious reflects the intentional design of a Creator who called His work "very good." When a man embraces that identity, he is empowered to lead boldly, serve faithfully, and leave a lasting legacy. As the pinnacle of God's creation, you are fearfully and wonderfully made (Ps. 139:14), crafted with intention, dignity, and divine purpose (Psalm 139:14). Your life is not an accident or an afterthought but a deliberate masterpiece, designed to reflect God's glory and fulfill His plan. God created men to be masculine. You were made on purpose for a purpose.

Throughout history, it was men who stepped forward in times of danger, leaving the safety of home to protect their families and communities. They carried the weight of responsibility, standing between those they loved and the threats that sought to harm them. This legacy of sacrifice reminds us that true strength is revealed in a willingness to defend, provide, and endure for the sake of others. It was men who had the responsibility to go to work to provide for their family. It takes real grit to put others above yourself, to seek first the Kingdom of God, and to live with purpose beyond self-interest. True strength is revealed in a man who can stand firm with courage while remaining tender, humble, and obedient to God's call. 2 Sam.

10:12 says, "Be of good courage, and let us be strong for our people and for the cities of our God." This is what it looks like to be a real man of God. You must be strong because the world and all the forces of evil will try to stop you from being the real man God called you to be.

| 6 |

"GO DEEPER"

There is an urgent need for men to reestablish and rebuild their foundation as men of God, grounded firmly in truth, obedience, and unwavering faith. When a man's life is anchored in God's Word, he stands strong against every storm and becomes a source of strength, leadership, and blessing to those around him. Today's generation desperately needs to see men of God living life as it was designed to be lived, lives anchored in truth, disciplined in character, and unwavering in faith. Words alone are no longer enough; authentic, consistent example is the loudest testimony a man can give. When men live rightly before God, they provide clarity, stability, and hope to a world starving for real leadership. They need us to be who God called us to be and not what the world pushes us to be. The enemy wants men to be feminized while God wants men to rise up and be mighty men of valor. The devil wants men to be jerks and tyrannical brutes whereas God wants all that you do to be done in love.

To have an effective influence in the world, you must stand firm and go deeper in establishing your understanding of who we are as a man of God. You must establish depth and stability in your life because a structure that rises high without a strong foundation is destined to collapse. This is why you must go deeper, not wider. Influence does not begin with position, visibility, or strength of personality - it begins with identity. Until a man knows who he is before God, his impact on the world will always be shallow, inconsistent, or misdirected. The world is not suffering from a lack of loud voices; it is suffering from a lack of rooted men - men who stand firm in truth and live from a settled understanding of who they are as men of God. A man who is easily shaken will never be trusted with lasting influence, because stability is the foundation of true leadership. While the world applauds flexibility and shifting convictions, God honors men who stand firm, remain rooted, and refuse to compromise when pressure comes.

Many men strive to influence crowds before they have allowed God to fully shape their own hearts. True authority is not produced by visibility or position, but by deep, quiet surrender to God's refining work. When God's influence runs deep within a man, his impact on others will naturally and powerfully follow. Depth always precedes reach. Going deeper means developing a disciplined inner life, allowing God to confront, refine, and correct us, choosing character over comfort, and seeking understanding, not just information. Shallow roots cannot sustain heavy fruit. If you want your life to carry weight, your relationship with God must carry depth. A man who does not know who he is in Christ will spend his life reacting instead of leading. Your identity is not based on career success, physical strength, financial provision, and social approval. It is grounded in your position as a son of God, your calling to reflect Christ, your responsibility to lead with integrity, and your submission to God's authority.

When your identity becomes clear, decisions become simpler. Temptation loses its power when a man knows what he stands for. The bottom line is your influence flows from your identity. True influence is not forced but is recognized in men who walk with conviction, speak with clarity, live with consistency, and serve with humility. Men who walk this way naturally impact the people around them. Influence flows from who a man is, not merely what he does. The world is not searching for flawless men, but for those whose strength is real, tested, and rooted in truth. When conviction, character, and conduct are aligned, influence follows naturally. This generation does not need men who blend in. It needs men who stand firm. It needs men who are willing to go deeper when others go softer, men who know who they are in God and refuse to surrender that identity. If you want to shape culture, raise families, strengthen churches, and leave a legacy, you must first know who you are as a man of God.

The effectiveness of a man's influence is never determined by how loudly he speaks or how widely he is known. It is determined by how deeply he is rooted. The world is filled with men who are visible, busy, and active, yet spiritually shallow - men attempting to change their surroundings without first allowing God to establish them inwardly. If a man does not know who he is, he will always be vulnerable to pressure. He will conform when he should confront, retreat when he should remain, and compromise when he should stand firm. Influence without identity is fragile. Authority without foundation is only temporary. To have an enduring influence in an unstable world, you must first stand firm in who you are as a man of God and then go deeper in that understanding until it becomes immovable. Scripture consistently calls men to firmness, stability, and endurance. They are to stand strong and hold fast. These are not passive instructions; they are commands that require strength and resolve.

Standing firm does not mean being harsh, rigid, or unteachable. It means being anchored. A firm man is not easily moved because his foundation is secure. He does not panic when culture shifts or crumble when pressure increases. Standing firm requires conviction that is rooted in the Word of God. It requires courage to resist compromise, a willingness to be misunderstood, and a commitment to truth over popularity. A man who stands firm provides stability not only for himself, but for everyone connected to him - his family, his church, and his community. Depth is the price of durability. It is not accidental. It is cultivated through intentional choices, spiritual discipline, and consistent obedience. Many men want influence without investment. They want strength without sacrifice. They want authority without accountability. But depth is costly, and there are no shortcuts. Going deeper requires time alone with God, honest self-examination, patience in growth, and perseverance through discomfort.

God often does His deepest work in seasons that feel slow, hidden, or even unproductive, because transformation at the root is rarely visible at the surface. In the quiet and unseen places, He is at work strengthening your foundation, shaping your character, and anchoring your faith deeper than circumstances can reach. What feels like delay is often divine preparation, where the roots grow strongest so lasting fruit can be borne in time. A man who refuses to go deeper with God may appear strong for a season, but his strength is only surface level. When pressure increases, what is shallow cannot sustain what is heavy. Without deep roots in God, collapse is not a possibility - it is inevitable. A man who embraces depth is anchored by conviction, not circumstance. When storms rise, he does not scramble for balance, because his roots run deeper than the winds that oppose him. Depth gives him the stability to endure pressure without losing his footing or his purpose.

Before God ever uses a man publicly, He first shapes him privately, where no applause is heard and no recognition is given. He does this because a man who seeks his assignment before his identity will misuse his authority. In the hidden places, character is forged, obedience is tested, and faith is deepened through quiet faithfulness. What is built in secret becomes the foundation God can trust when He brings a man into public purpose. Before David wore a crown, he tended sheep. Before Moses confronted Pharaoh, he spent years in obscurity. Before Jesus began His public ministry, He was affirmed in His identity as the Son. God is intentional about doing things in divine order. He is never random or rushed; He works with divine precision, accomplishing each thing in its appointed time and order. What may feel like delay to us is often preparation, as He builds the foundation before revealing the fulfillment. When God orders the steps, nothing is missing, nothing is premature, and nothing is wasted.

A man who understands who he is before God does not chase power; he accepts responsibility as a sacred trust. Grounded in his identity, he leads with humility, knowing that authority is given to serve, not to dominate. His strength is steady and disciplined, shaped by obedience rather than ego. Because he answers first to God, he carries responsibility with courage, restraint, and unwavering integrity. Your identity as a man of God begins with sonship, not servanthood. Before God ever asks you to do anything for Him, He establishes who you are to Him: a son loved, accepted, and secure. When a man serves from sonship rather than striving for approval, his obedience flows from intimacy, not obligation. Before God entrusts you with authority over others, He first requires accountability over your own life - your motives, obedience, and faithfulness when no one else is watching. Authority in God's kingdom is not granted to those who seek position, but to those who have learned to answer fully to Him.

Being faithful always comes before being fruitful. God never prioritizes what you produce over who you become. In the Kingdom of God, faithfulness is the soil in which fruitfulness grows. 1 Cor. 4:2 says, "Moreover it is required in stewards, that a man be found faithful." God is not first looking for results; He is looking for reliability, obedience, and trustworthiness. Fruit is the outcome of faithfulness, not the starting point. It's faithfulness that builds character that can bring forth fruitfulness in God's kingdom. Faithfulness means showing up, standing firm, and obeying God even when nothing appears to be happening. Many people want the harvest without enduring the season of planting. But scripture shows us that God measures obedience long before He multiplies results. God does not promote potential; He promotes proven faithfulness. When you chase fruitfulness without faithfulness, you'll become anxious, driven, and discouraged. But when you pursue faithfulness, fruitfulness follows naturally.

Fruit without character leads to collapse. God is patient because He is protecting us from being crushed by what we are not yet ready to carry. Faithfulness develops discipline, endurance, integrity, humility, and trust in God rather than self. These traits are not optional; they are load-bearing pillars for long-term fruitfulness. Gal. 6:9 says, "Let us not grow weary in well doing; for in due season we will reap, if we faint not." The harvest comes in due season, not in rushed seasons. Eventually, God brings increase. He always does. But when He does, it comes without striving, without manipulation, and without burnout. Fruit born from faithfulness is sustainable, God-ordained, protected by grace, and anchored in purpose. Do not rush the harvest and do not abandon obedience because results are slow. God is not ignoring your faithfulness. He is building a foundation strong enough to hold what He plans to give you. Be faithful first and fruitfulness will follow as God brings lasting increase in His perfect time.

When your identity in Christ is settled in your heart, your calling becomes clear. Men who do not know who they are will spend their lives performing. They chase validation, applause, and acceptance, often at the cost of integrity. But a man who is secure in his identity does not need to impress - he needs only to be faithful. True influence is quiet but powerful. It is seen in consistency, reliability, and character. A rooted man may not always be the loudest in the room, but he is often the most trusted. His influence shows up in the stability of his home, the integrity of his work, the faithfulness of his walk, and the example he sets for other men. Men who are rooted create environments where others feel safe, supported, and strengthened. Their lives preach louder than their words. Standing firm and going deeper is not optional. It is essential. This generation needs men who know who they are in Christ, men who are willing to slow down, dig deep, and allow God to establish them from the inside out.

If you desire to influence the world, you must first allow God to define you, refine you, and anchor you. When your identity is clear and roots are deep, influence becomes inevitable and enduring. You were made in the image of God (Gen. 1:27), which means your life carries divine purpose, dignity, and value. You are not an accident or an afterthought - you are a living reflection designed to reveal God's character to the world. A creation will always reflect the nature of its creator. A book will reflect the nature of its author, and a building will reflect the nature of the architect. Because you were made by God, you are here to reflect His nature. You're here to walk as Jesus walked. Understanding your origin will greatly impact the decisions you'll make. When you know where you came from, you'll automatically know who to act like. This is why the devil tries to deceive people by telling them they evolved from monkeys. If you believe you came from a beast, you'll act like a beast.

You are called to reflect God in your conduct - living with excellence, righteousness, and love - because the God you represent is truly awesome. God is a faithful Protector, an unfailing Provider, a merciful Redeemer, and the master Builder who restores and strengthens every part of our lives. God is gentle yet unbreakably strong. He is tender with the broken, but fearsome to anything that threatens what He loves. He brings mercy and help to the helpless, and He brings swift, righteous justice to evil. He's loving and He's dangerous. He brings help to the helpless and justice to evil. He is joyful and He is very generous. He is patient and He is active. He is creative and He is careful. He is slow to anger and quick to forgive. He's affectionate and effective. He is a mighty warrior and a loving Father. Every good thing comes from Him. The more you act like God and the more your character aligns with His nature, the more your relationships, influence, and environment are lifted to a higher level.

There is a deep yearning in the heart of every man to know that his life has meaning, that his presence in this world is not accidental or insignificant. He longs to know that there is a reason for him to be alive, that he matters to God, to others, and to a purpose greater than himself. When a man discovers the reason he was created, that inner ache is replaced with clarity, strength, and the resolve to live intentionally. In His grace, God has lovingly placed a calling on your life - one that is not random but intentionally designed by His hand. Your purpose flows from that grace, empowering you to live with meaning, direction, and confidence as you walk in what He has ordained. 2 Tim. 1:9 says God "called us with a holy calling according to His own purpose and grace." To understand your calling, you must examine what God declared in the Garden of Eden before sin distorted purpose. In Eden, God revealed humanity's original assignment making your calling a restoration of that first divine intent.

In the beginning, man was created to reflect His image, steward His creation, and walk with Him. God blessed Adam and Eve and said to them, "Be fruitful and increase in number, fill the earth and subdue it" (Gen. 1:28). God commissioned them to work, to build, to multiply, to overcome, to conquer. God is calling you to do the same thing. He didn't create you to play golf all day. Every man carries within him a natural, God-given drive be successful, to advance and get ahead, to build and achieve more than yesterday. That inner ambition is not accidental - it is the engine that propels him forward, calling him to rise, lead, and leave a meaningful mark. Every man carries the desire to do something that matters - to build, lead, and leave a mark that outlives him. Deep within his heart is the longing to shape the world around him for the better, to create something meaningful that reflects purpose, courage, and legacy. That drive comes from God, and you must use it for the glory of God.

There is no man without a calling and a purpose. God did not create you by accident or without intention. You were designed with divine precision to do something that matters, something that leaves an impact beyond yourself. When you discover and commit to that God-given purpose, your life moves from existing to truly counting. Every man is born with ambition, drive, and the desire to achieve - but ambition itself is not the problem. The defining question is whether that ambition will be surrendered to God's glory or consumed by self-promotion and personal gain. In the end, you will serve someone with your life; the only question is whether it will be God's purpose or your own. Rise up and be a real man! Use what God has given you to glorify Him and advance His kingdom in the world. You will do incredible things with your life if you'll be a good steward of your talents, resources, and time. You'll impact your family, your church, and your community. You'll leave a legacy that really makes a difference.

God has already promised His help toward your success, but His promises are activated through obedience and diligence. When you follow His direction with a willing heart and commit yourself to working very, very hard, you align your effort with His favor. In that alignment, God causes it to go well with you and brings lasting results that honor Him. Deut. 8:18 says, "Remember the Lord your God. He is the one who gives you power to be successful." Success is not self-generated but God-given, flowing from His grace rather than our own strength. Remembering the Lord keeps us humble, grateful, and rightly aligned, recognizing Him as the true source behind every achievement and provision. To succeed, you must act like you're working for Jesus. He's the one you labor for. To be successful, all you have to do is listen to God and do what He tells you to do. Go deeper with Him knowing that blessings follow obedience. When you follow His ways, you'll experience His benefits. You'll be successful in all you do.

| 7 |

"BE WATCHFUL"

In today's world, more and more females are being replaced by males who act like women. Long-standing distinctions between masculinity and femininity are increasingly blurred, creating confusion about identity, purpose, and roles. The culture today increasingly confuses identity and responsibility, diminishing the unique strength of women while undermining the purpose and accountability of men. When womanhood is blurred and manhood is vilified, families lose stability and children lose clear models of love, discipline, and security. A society that weakens its men and erases its women ultimately fractures the very foundation on which healthy generations are built. Men have long been the target of the enemy, but the ultimate goal of the evil one is to get the children. Why? Because the children of today will be the leaders of tomorrow. The devil knows that in order to get control of the children, he has to take out the men. This is why the world today is telling men to step back, sit down, and shut up!

What's sad in all this is that most men are listening to them. Never before has the need been greater for the men of God to step up and act like men who are strong in conviction, grounded in truth, and unashamed of righteousness. In an age of confusion and compromise, God is calling men to lead with courage, serve with humility, and stand firm on His Word. The future of our families, churches, and communities depends on men who will answer that call without hesitation. The term "act like men" in 1 Cor. 16:13 is the Greek word "andrizomai" and this is the only place in the New Testament this word is used. The word means 'to show oneself a man and to be courageous like a man should be.' To show oneself a man is to take responsibility without retreat, to stand firm when pressure comes, and to lead with conviction rather than convenience. True courage is not the absence of fear, but the resolve to act rightly in spite of it, choosing obedience, integrity, and strength of character.

A man proves himself courageous when he refuses to shrink back, meets adversity head-on, and lives faithfully according to what he knows is right. Through the inspiration of the Holy Spirit, Paul challenges men to assume their God-given responsibility to act like men. In five clear and crisp commands, Paul lays before you the duties of a real man of God. The commands of 1 Cor. 16:13,14 were meant to be put into practice immediately and lived out continually. Vigilance, steadfast faith, courage, and strength are not occasional virtues but a continual posture of a disciplined Christian life. When these commands are lived out daily and motivated by love, they produce a faith that is both resilient in trials and powerful in influence. These commands are all military terms and are imperatives for a victorious life as a real man of God. They are not suggestions but marching orders, demanding immediate obedience and continual practice for those determined to live and lead triumphantly.

Four of these have reference to spiritual foes and perils, while the last one sums up our duty to one another. First, to be a real man and to act like a man, 1 Cor. 16:13 says you must "be watchful." All men must stand as sentinels on guard, faithfully maintaining their post with vigilance and resolve, knowing that what they protect matters. They must manifest courage not only in moments of conflict, but in daily obedience, discipline, and unwavering commitment to what is right. In doing so, they become strong, forged through responsibility, tested by endurance, and established as dependable defenders of truth and legacy. They must maintain a posture of vigilance and sensitivity to spiritual dangers and attacks, against desertion from the truth, and against moral weakening. To "be watchful" means 'to take heed lest through remission and indolence some destructive calamity suddenly overtakes us.' This is why 1 Thess. 5:6 says, "Therefore let us not sleep, as others do, but let us watch and be sober."

Men, you need to stay alert like a watchman who stands guard on a wall that surrounds a city with eyes fixed on every movement and threat. What a man allows to enter his mind, home, and heart will ultimately determine the safety and strength of everything entrusted to him. Vigilance is not optional - it is the responsibility of a man who intends to protect his calling, his family, and his future. The well-being of your family rests heavily on your willingness to stand as a man who is alert, engaged, and unwilling to be careless with what God has entrusted to you. A watchful man sees danger before it arrives, guards his home with wisdom and courage, and takes responsibility for the safety, direction, and spiritual health of those he loves. Don't let the enemy breach the walls of your home. Know the culture's influence on your family. Children today are being bombarded by things that destroy how they think about themselves and others. They're confused and their innocence is being stolen from them.

In today's world, children are being exposed to pornography at under ten years of age. It's all a click away on the phone they carry. They're being told their gender identity can be surgically altered without their parent's permission. This is why it is imperative that you remain watchful and actively protect your children. The world is filled with influences and dangers that seek to shape them before they are strong enough to discern truth for themselves. Your vigilance, guidance, and example create a covering that guards their hearts, minds, and future. Don't let them have a phone when they're not in your presence. Keep watch over the programs they watch and the music they listen to. Be careful about the friends you let them have/ It's your responsibility to do this. You can't be a watchman if you don't look at what your children are doing and respond accordingly. They may get mad at you but that's okay. You're not a real parent until your children do get mad at you. Be a watchman and stay at your post.

A real man understands that both he and his family live under constant threat from the enemy, for as 1 Cor. 15:30 declares, "We stand in jeopardy every hour." Because danger is real and relentless, complacency is not an option for a man who has been entrusted with leadership and protection. Therefore, he remains vigilant - watching, praying, and standing guard - knowing that alertness is an essential expression of love and responsibility. To be watchful means to remain alert to the influences shaping the world around you, discerning what strengthens faith and what quietly erodes it. It also means intentionally examining the spiritual condition of your own heart and remaining attentive to the souls of those God has entrusted to your care. In Mark 13:37 Jesus said, "And what I say to you, I say to all: Watch!" This is a command all men should be obeying. The Message Bible says, "Stay at your post. Keep watch." This command requires strict attention and obedience by all men.

The Greek word for "watch" is "gregoreuo" and Jesus used this word fourteen times in the gospels. He said in Matt. 24:42, "Watch therefore, for you do not know what hour the Lord is coming." Luke 12:37 says, "Blessed are those servants whom the master, when he comes, will find watching." This is telling us that true blessings belong to those who remain alert, faithful, and fully engaged in the Master's work, even when no one is watching. A watchful servant lives each day with purpose and expectation, knowing that readiness is not passive waiting but active obedience. Jesus said to His disciples, "My soul is exceedingly sorrowful, even to death. Stay here and watch with Me" (Matt. 26:28). His words call us to a vigilant, compassionate faith - one that does not withdraw in times of pain but stays present, prayerful, and watchful with Him. Sad to say, His disciples did not watch but instead fell asleep. As a consequence, they failed miserably (Matt. 26:56). May you never do the same. Be watchful at all times.

If you fail to keep watch and warn others when danger is approaching, you will share the responsibility for the harm that follows. God makes it clear that silence in the face of known danger is not innocence, but accountability. According to Ezek. 33:6, neglecting your duty to watch and warn places the burden of consequence squarely on you. Biblically speaking, watching out for others is never passive - it is an attentive, energetic, and focused posture of the soul. Scripture presents watching as spiritual alertness: eyes open, mind engaged, and heart prepared to act when God speaks or moves. To watch is to live on guard with expectation, disciplined awareness, and purposeful readiness rather than casual observation. Watching is seeing with the intention to engage, not merely to observe. It is awareness that prepares the mind and positions the will for action. When danger is seen approaching, true watching responds decisively, because vigilance without action is negligence.

All men of God are like soldiers posted on a wall, standing watch while others rest safely within. Their calling is to see what others cannot yet see and to confront danger before it breaches the gates. When faithful men hold their ground, families, churches, and future generations remain protected and secure. Men who are entrusted to watch over others must remain alert and vigilant, understanding that attentiveness is the first line of protection against danger and compromise. They must stand steadfast, courageous, and strong, refusing to retreat when pressure, fear, or adversity arises. Above all, they must be united in purpose and spirit, knowing that strength is multiplied when men stand together in unwavering commitment. In other words, they must act like men, real men! The greater the danger, the greater the vigilance, because real threats demand heightened awareness and disciplined focus. When the stakes rise, wisdom calls you to watch more closely and stand more resolutely.

You're on that wall to make sure the enemy does no harm to those you're assigned to protect. If the enemy can take you out, then those under your care will be defenseless. If the devil takes you out, then everyone suffers. When there is no man standing watch on the wall, women and children bear the cost of that absence in ways that were never God's intent. A man's failure to rise into his God-given role of protector and guardian creates a vacuum where strength, covering, and responsibility were meant to stand. 1 Peter 5:8 (MSG) says, "The devil is poised to pounce, and would like nothing better than to catch you napping. Keep your guard up." Spiritual laziness prevents men from acting like men. This is why the men of God today need to wake up. Never let your guard down but remain vigilant against our mortal enemies: the world, the flesh, and the devil. The Christian life is one of constant danger and trouble. If you are going to be victorious, you must be watchful and alert at all times.

The Greek word "gregoreuo" means 'to be watchful or to refrain from physical sleep.' It means 'to be on the alert in a constant state of readiness to respond to the attacks of the enemy.' Every man is called to live alert, standing watch with disciplined awareness, knowing that the enemy looks for moments of complacency to strike. Constant readiness is not fear - it is responsibility, the steady posture of a man prepared to defend truth, protect others, and respond without hesitation when the battle comes. It means to give strict attention to, to be active, to take heed lest through neglect some destructive calamity suddenly overtakes you. The Greeks used this word to describe people carefully crossing a river while stepping on slippery stones. If they did not pay strict attention to their steps, they would end up in the water. The idea is to stay alert and be cautious for the spiritual war we are in demands vigilance at all times.1 Cor. 10:12 says, "Let him who thinks he stands take heed lest he fall."

The term "wake up" appears 22 times in the New Testament and consistently speaks to a call for spiritual alertness rather than physical awakening. It urges all men to remain attentive, discerning, and ready - fully aware of God's truth, His timing, and their responsibility to live purposefully. Real men are called to wake up - to be spiritually alert, not drifting through life unaware of the battles, opportunities, and responsibilities before them. They keep their eyes open and their hearts engaged, paying attention to what God is doing in them, around them, and through them. With their head on a swivel, they discern the times, guard what matters, and stand ready to act with wisdom, courage, and conviction. Don't be complacent but constantly be on the lookout for threats that may come your way. There is a thief who comes to steal, kill, and destroy and Jesus said in Matt. 24:43, "If a homeowner knew exactly when a burglar was coming, he would keep watch and not permit his house to be broken into."

When men are not watchful, the enemy slips in quietly and wreaks havoc like a fox in a hen house, stealing peace, unity, and order. 1 Peter 5:8 (NLT) says, "Stay alert! Watch out for your great enemy, the devil. He prowls around like a roaring lion, looking for someone to devour." A charging lion can cover over a hundred yards in just three seconds. Don't underestimate your enemy. He is fast, clever, and ruthlessly effective. He studies your weaknesses, waits for moments of complacency, and strikes where discipline is lacking. Weak men become easy prey, but vigilant, strengthened men become impossible targets. A lack of spiritual vigilance leaves homes exposed, allowing compromise, confusion, and division to take root unchecked. Strong men stay alert, stand guard in prayer and truth, and protect what God has entrusted to them. Remain at your post and be watchful at all times. Always be vigilant to keep your guard up because you never know when the enemy will strike.

The devil is profoundly deceptive and rarely attacks head-on. More often, he looks for unguarded places, slipping in quietly through the back door of compromise dressed as an angel of light. He disguises his intentions, presenting temptation as harmless, reasonable, or even righteous. That is why discernment is essential to recognize the counterfeit light-bearer for who he truly is. The devil never takes a day off, and neither should you. Never let your guard down because spiritual opposition is relentless. This is why spiritual vigilance must be constant. A spiritual sabbatical is not rest; it is an opening for an attack because drifting always begins when discipline is paused. Stay prayed up, Word-filled, and alert every day because consistency is the price of victory. If you've been saved for a while, it's easy to rest on your laurels and fail to move forward spiritually. You will live beneath your potential because you will not exert the effort required to grow. You will stop striving, stop stretching, and stop advancing.

The life of a Christian man of God is marked by constant growth and transformation as he is daily shaped by truth, obedience, and grace. He does not remain who he was, because walking with God demands continual renewal and a relentless pursuit of becoming more like Christ. Keep pressing forward because if you keep looking back, you'll start going back. That's why Jesus said, "Remember Lot's wife" (Luke 17:32). Don't look back or live in the past. Don't be crippled by past mistakes and moral failures because they are all forgiven in Christ. Also, past victories were never meant to be permanent resting places. A man of God moves forward with humility and faith, pressing on toward what God is doing now and calling him into next. Paul said in Phil. 3;13,14 says, "One thing I do, forgetting those things which are behind and reaching forward to those things which are ahead. I press on to reach the end of the race and receive the heavenly prize for which God, through Jesus Christ, is calling us."

Keep growing spiritually every single day by intentionally pursuing God, sharpening your character, and refusing to settle for yesterday's faith. Always take time to reflect on what it truly means to be a real man of God - one who walks in humility, obedience, courage, and unwavering devotion to Christ. The stronger you are spiritually, the clearer your vision becomes and the steadier your position as a watchman. A disciplined prayer life, attentiveness to God's Word, and sensitivity to the Spirit sharpen your ability to discern danger before it arrives. Devastation is never sudden but is the predictable result of failing to keep watch when we were called to stand alert and watchful. We are in a war and the devil will destroy you and your family if he possibly can. Great pain in life can often be avoided when you remain spiritually alert and intentionally keep watch over the things that matter most. Vigilance protects what is valuable, while neglect quietly opens the door to loss, regret, and unnecessary suffering.

Be vigilant! Stay awake! The ability to keep watch is inside of you. You were created for this. You were built with a unique sense of awareness, designed by God to perceive more than just what is obvious on the surface. This awareness allows you to recognize what is happening around you so you can respond with wisdom rather than reaction. When you learn to pay attention, you position yourself to discern God's direction, avoid unnecessary harm, and walk intentionally in your calling. You'll know on the inside when something isn't right. You're alert to the wiles and schemes of the enemy. Stay awake! If you snooze, you lose. Adam didn't keep watch and look at the condition the world is in today. God makes it very clear that there is a specific way men are supposed to act and it all starts with being watchful. Real men are committed to pursuing purpose, always being watchful while leading and loving the people entrusted to them. It's good to be a man, it's even better to act like one.

| 8 |

"STAND FIRM"

Everybody wins when men act like men. When men are strong in character, steady in responsibility, and faithful in conviction, families are safer, communities are stronger, and leadership becomes trustworthy. God designed men to stand, serve, protect, and lead with humility and courage, not to shrink back or surrender their calling. The world is desperate for men who know who they are and are willing to live it out with integrity and resolve. Don't let fear, failure, culture, or compromise stop you from being the man God called you to be.1 Cor. 16:13 tells men to always be watchful. It then says to "stand firm in the faith." This is a military term - a masculine command - calling a man to hold his ground without compromise. It declares that when it comes to faith, retreat is not an option and surrender is not permitted. You are commanded to stand firm, yield nothing, and give the enemy not a single inch. Great faith is the product of standing firm in the faith. When you don't cave in, great faith is produced.

Standing firm in faith is how God grows you from little faith to great faith with each test strengthening your spiritual resolve. When you refuse to retreat, the small victories matter; they are the training ground where lions and bears are defeated in private. In time, that same unshakable stance positions you to face and conquer the giants that once seemed impossible. Great faith is forged on the battlefields of life, when pressure is real, the stakes are high, and your very existence feels threatened. In those moments, faith ceases to be theoretical and becomes a life-preserving force, rising strong because there is no other place left to stand. Great testimonies are the result of standing firm in great tests. Great triumph can only come from great trials. When you stand firm, every stumbling block will become a steppingstone. Every opposition will become an opportunity. Standing firm causes you to walk fearlessly, run confidently, and live victoriously. When you stand firm in the faith, you'll go from glory to glory.

Heb. 11:6 declares that "without faith it is impossible to please God" thus establishing faith as the foundation of our relationship with Him. Faith is not a passive belief but an active trust that anchors our obedience, endurance, and hope. This is why Paul commands us to stand firm in the faith. He knows that a steadfast faith keeps us grounded, unmoved, and pleasing to God in every season. Faith steps forward in obedience and trust for faith is the victory that overcomes the world (1 John 5:4). True faith moves before the evidence appears, activating the power of God in real time. Miracles are not the requirement for faith; they are the result of faith put into action. If you'll stand firm when trials come your way, you won't bow, bend, or burn. You'll stand strong victoriously. It is God's will that all men have unshakable faith, a faith that is anchored in the Lord Jesus Christ. A real man understands that everything comes from the Lord. He looks to the Lord for strength, provision, and protection.

The gospel message declares that through Christ we are brought into oneness with God, no longer distant or separated. In Him, God is not standing against us in judgment but standing with us in love and purpose. This unity means His strength supports our weakness, and His victory becomes our hope. To know the gospel is to know that God is on our side, working in us and for us to bring life, restoration, and redemption. Ps. 23:4 says, "Though I walk through the valley of the shadow of death, I will fear no evil for You are with me." This causes a real man to stand firm in absolute confidence because he knows God is on his side. And because God is on your side, you can be strong in the Lord and in the power of His might (Eph. 6:10). A man who stands firm in the faith is anchored by shoes forged in conviction, gripping the unshakable truth of God's promises and keeping him steady no matter the terrain. Rooted in his relationship with the Almighty, a real man does not fall or retreat under pressure.

Eph. 6:13,14 calls us to a resolute posture of faith saying, "Having done all to stand, stand therefore." This is a command to remain immovable when the battle has exhausted your strength and quitting seems justified. Standing firm is not passive. It is an active refusal to surrender ground the enemy has not earned. If you stand your ground and do not quit, the outcome is already decided. You win. Every man on the planet will face trials and challenges designed to test the depth of his commitment to Christ and the authenticity of his faith. These moments are not meant to break him, but to refine his character, strengthen his resolve, and reveal whether his allegiance is rooted in unwavering devotion. Hold on when the going gets tough. Dig your heels in and remain consistent as you face hardship, danger, persecution, and conflict. Prov. 3:5,6 says, "Trust in the Lord with all your heart, and lean not on your own understanding. In all your ways acknowledge Him, and He will direct your paths."

Receive these words and allow your spirit to be charged up with fresh strength and confidence in your faith. Stand your ground when circumstances press against you, refusing to retreat from what God has promised. Trust fully in the Lord, knowing He is faithful to sustain you, defend you, and bring you through in victory. When the enemy attacks you, remember the promise of Is. 59:19 says, "Like a flood the Spirit of the Lord will lift up a standard against him." What rises against you is never greater than what rises for you, because God Himself stands in defense of those who trust Him. Even when every circumstance seems stacked against you, choose to place your confidence in the Lord, knowing that He remains sovereign and faithful. Stand firm in your faith, because steadfast trust positions you to see God's strength revealed in the midst of adversity. Sometimes the most courageous thing you can do is stand. Resist the urge to veer off course, to back off, to run away in the face of fear.

When the enemy shows up like Goliath did, plant your feet, fix your focus, and refuse to retreat from the ground God has given you. Stand firm in faith, unmoved by intimidation or fear, knowing that the battle belongs to the Lord. As you hold your position in obedience and trust, God Himself will bring the deliverance. The term "stand firm" appears eight times in the New Testament and it means to 'be steadfast and immovable.' The Bible tells us to stand firm in the faith (1 Cor. 16:13), stand firm in one spirit (Phil. 1:27), and stand firm in the Lord (Phil. 4:1). "Stand firm" means 'to hold your ground, maintain a position, remain upright, persist, persevere, and don't give up.' 1 Peter 5:8 says, "Be alert and of a sober mind. Your enemy the devil prowls around like a roaring lion looking for someone to devour." We stand firm by staying alert keeping our eyes wide open. When we live watchful and disciplined, the enemy loses the element of surprise, and his attacks are exposed before they can take hold.

Being a real man of God does not mean you are exempt from trials and hardship. On the contrary. In fact, it often places you directly in their path. Jesus said in John 16:33, "In the world you will have tribulation; but be of good cheer, I have overcome the world." God uses pressure, resistance, and adversity to forge strength, deepen faith, and refine character. A man of God is not defined by the absence of struggle, but by his willingness to stand firm, trust God, and endure faithfully through it. 1 Cor. 15:58 says you are to stand firm in your faith, refusing to be shaken by adversity, doubt, or opposition. Let nothing move you from the truth God has established in your heart, knowing that His promises are unchanging. Give yourself fully to the work of the Lord, confident that every act of obedience and faithfulness carries eternal value. The Greek term "stand firm" implies stability and firmness. Become like a tree standing firm against a strong wind or a spouse supporting an ailing partner.

The journey of a man is rarely easy, marked by trials that test his resolve and opposition that seeks to weaken his purpose. Yet it is in these moments of pressure - through persecution, resistance, and hardship - that true character is revealed and forged. A man must stand firm, anchored in conviction, refusing to retreat, knowing that endurance today produces strength, maturity, and victory tomorrow. No matter what you face, remain anchored and fixed on Jesus, for He is the unchanging foundation when everything around you is shifting. Storms may rage and pressures may increase, but Christ remains steady, faithful, and immovable. When your heart is fastened to Him, you will not drift, break, or be overcome - you will stand. There is no back-up plan and no fallback option other than rock-solid faith in a rock-solid Savior. Ps. 62:1 says, "My soul finds rest in God alone; my salvation comes from Him. He alone is my rock and my salvation. He is my fortress; I will never be shaken."

Jesus once asked His disciples if they would abandon Him like others had done and Peter responded, "Lord, to whom shall we go? You have the words of eternal life" (John 6:68). When trouble comes, do not withdraw from Jesus - draw nearer to Him. Trials are not signals to retreat, but invitations to anchor your life more deeply in His presence and promises. Running to Christ in the storm is how your faith is strengthened and how you stand firm, unshaken and secure. Jesus Christ is the only sure, solid foundation in this cold and evil world, a world that is forever changing for the worse. Jesus Christ is the source of our strength, empowering us to stand firm, press forward, and overcome every challenge we face. 2 Cor. 2:14 declares, "Now thanks be unto God, which causes us to triumph in Christ." He faithfully leads us in victory. He is a real man's steadfast anchor. Stand firm in the Lord and be unshakable. Believe the words of Ex. 14:14, "The Lord will fight for you, and you shall hold your peace."

The Greek word "steko" pictures an army that refuses to retreat even though it is being assaulted by the enemy. The only way to stand firm in a shifting world is to be standing on a rock-solid, unshakable foundation. When storms come - and they always do - only what is firmly anchored will remain upright and unmoved. A life built on truth, obedience, and unwavering faith will not collapse when pressure, opposition, or adversity arrives. Let Jesus be the center of your life - the fixed point from which every decision, priority, and purpose flows. When He is your foundation, you stand on a rock that does not shift with culture, circumstances, or storms. Life may shake what surrounds you, but it cannot move what you are built upon. Rooted in Christ, you remain steady, confident, and unshaken no matter what comes. Ps. 125:1 says, "Those who trust in the Lord shall be as Mount Zion, which cannot be moved, but abides forever." 1 Thess. 3:8, "For now we really live, if you stand firm in the Lord."

Col. 4:12 says you should "stand perfect and fully assured in all the will of God." The Passion Translation says you should "grow and mature, standing complete and perfect in God's plan for your lives." Growth in God is not optional - it is a calling to move beyond beginnings and mature into the fullness of who He designed you to be. As you grow, your faith becomes rooted, your character refined, and your life aligned with His purpose rather than your own preferences. When you stand mature, complete, and fully surrendered, you are positioned to walk confidently in God's perfect plan for your life. Jude 24 says, "Now to Him who is able to keep you from stumbling, and to make you stand in the presence of His glory blameless with great joy." The Message Bible says, "And now to Him who can keep you on your feet, standing tall in His bright presence, fresh and celebrating." Get rid of self-reliance and rely wholly on the Lord who alone can provide the supernatural enablement that allows you to stand firm.

The only way to stand firm spiritually is by remaining in constant communion with the Lord because strength is sustained by relationship, not resolve alone. When prayer, obedience, and attentiveness to God's voice become a daily rhythm, faith is continually reinforced against pressure and compromise. A life anchored in ongoing fellowship with the Lord is not easily shaken, because it draws stability from an unchanging source. Be steadfast like an immovable object, anchored firmly in truth and unshaken by pressure, opposition, or changing circumstances. Boldly embrace the Word of God as your final authority, holding it with conviction rather than convenience. When faith refuses to waver, it becomes a foundation that cannot be moved and a testimony that cannot be silenced. A cultural tidal wave is sweeping over the entire planet. Its purpose is to wipe away all godly virtues. It hates the truth and celebrates sin. You only have two options. You can go with the flow or stand firmly in the faith.

More than ever, you need to stand your ground because the pressures to compromise have never been stronger. When you refuse to retreat, you don't just protect your own integrity; you become a steady landmark others can look to when everything else is shifting. Draw a line in the sand with boldness and courage. Rise up in faith and declare with boldness the words of Is. 54:17, "No weapon formed against you shall prosper." Is. 40:29 says, "He gives power to the family and to him who has no might He increases strength." Stand firm in the faith and Jesus will keep your feet from being swept away. He'll place you on solid ground. In Jesus, all doubts are destroyed and all fears are cast away. The wiles of the enemy will be ineffective and useless against you. You won't be swept away by the tide of fear because you are anchored in Christ Jesus. When trouble comes your way, you won't panic or lose hope because in Jesus you have a spirit of power, love, and a sound mind (2 Tim. 1:7).

Jesus said in Luke 11:21, "When a strong man, fully armed, guards his own house, his possessions are safe." You are the gatekeeper of your home, entrusted with the responsibility to protect what God has placed under your care. You stand at the door, discerning what is allowed to enter and what must be kept out. An enemy does not need an invitation when vigilance is absent, but he cannot cross a guarded threshold. When you stand watch with conviction, wisdom, and courage, your home becomes a place of peace, strength, and spiritual security. You keep watch and you stand firm. You must do this because the man who doesn't protect his family is worse than an unbeliever (1 Tim. 5:8). You are called to stand and persevere in spite of persecution, to withstand storms without wavering. A real man resists the enemy and runs his race with endurance. He stands firm and continues the course without cowering in fear being confident that what God has established in him cannot be overthrown.

Thankfully, the Lord is your shield and defense (Ps. 91:4). His Word is a lamp to your feet and a light to your path (Ps. 119:105). Stand firm in the faith, even when circumstances attempt to shake your confidence, for God honors unwavering trust. When you refuse to retreat or compromise, He moves decisively on your behalf. The Lord sees every scheme, plan, and hidden plot of the enemy. In His perfect timing, He will overthrow them all and establish His purpose in your life. David said to Goliath, "The battle is the Lord's, and he will give you into our hands" (1 Sam. 17:47). Ps. 124:2,3 (MSG) says, "If God hadn't been for us when everyone went against us, we would have been swallowed alive." Stand firm when your heart is heavy and the way forward feels hidden from your sight. When you have prayed and believed, when you have done all you know to do, do not retreat. Having done all to stand, stand therefore, trusting that God is working even when you cannot yet perceive the outcome.

Ex. 14:13 says, "Do not be afraid. Stand firm and you will see the deliverance the Lord will bring you today." To stand firm, you must first have a clear vision of where God is leading you, because stability is born from purpose. When you ask Him in faith, He is faithful to reveal direction, clarity, and timing. God does not leave His people wandering - He gives a divine road map to those who seek Him and are willing to follow. Godly vision is powerful because it gives pain a purpose, transforming suffering into preparation rather than punishment. When you understand why you are going through the pain, it no longer weakens you - it strengthens your resolve and sharpens your faith. A man who knows the reason behind the struggle will stand firmer, endure longer, and go farther than one who walks without vision. If you have a vision for the future, you'll be able to stand firm and endure the crisis you're in. When you focus on God's plan for your life, you'll overcome the urge to quit and give up.

Direction has always been more important than speed, because movement without purpose is simply wasted effort. You can go fast but if you're going in the wrong direction, you'll get nowhere fast. You can move fast, stay busy, and feel productive, yet still end up no closer to where you were meant to be. But when the direction you are going is aligned with truth, purpose, and wisdom, even steady steps will carry you farther than reckless acceleration ever could. A clear vision provides guardrails for your life, keeping you aligned with what truly matters and protecting you from distractions that waste your time and energy. When your vision is strong, it becomes a filter that clarifies what deserves your focus and what must be left behind. You can't do everything, but vision tells you the very thing God wants you to do. It will give you direction for your life. It will tell you where to go and where not to go. It will cause you to stand firm in the faith, the very thing that makes all dreams possible.

| 9 |

"BEHIND ENEMY LINES"

You were born into a war. Real men of God today live as exiles in a foreign land, standing firm in faith and conviction much like Daniel did in Babylon. Though surrounded by a culture that opposes God's ways, they remain uncompromised, loyal to the Lord, courageous in obedience, and unshaken in purpose. We live in a world that is steadily drifting away from godly morals and values, celebrating compromise while rejecting truth. In such a time, believers are called to stand firm, live distinctly, and reflect God's unchanging standards through both conviction and compassion. The world today is in a darker and more broken condition than at any other time, marked by confusion, corruption, and open rebellion against what is right. Yet in the midst of this rising evil, God is still raising up real men - men of conviction, courage, and unshakable faith - who refuse to bow to the spirit of the age. These men stand as watchmen and warriors, shining the light of truth and righteousness when it is needed most.

We are in a war - not one fought with flesh and blood, but a continual battle for truth, faith, and obedience. This is not a moment for retreat or hesitation; it is a call to stand, advance, and contend with unwavering boldness and God-given confidence. Those who know who they are and whose they are fight every day with courage, resolve, and unshakable trust in the victory already secured. We fight for what's right. We fight with the end in mind. We may be outnumbered but our Commander-In-Chief is the King of kings and Lord of lords. Dan. 4:17 says, "For this has been decreed by the messengers so that everyone may know that the Most High rules over the kingdom of the world." Make no mistake about it, the sovereign God is still on the throne ruling over all no matter how dark or chaotic the world becomes. Because His authority has not changed, and never will change, we are called to rise up and stand firm in the faith, confident that our trust rests in a King who will never fail.

Yes, the world is predominantly evil, but God chose to put you here in the midst of it all. He has placed you behind enemy lines. The world you were born into is not morally neutral. Scripture does not soften this reality, and neither should you. Darkness is not an occasional visitor here but is a prevailing influence. Systems are bent away from God, appetites are trained toward selfishness, and truth is routinely exchanged for convenience. From the opening pages of scripture to the final warnings of Revelation, the Bible consistently describes a world that resists God's authority. Jesus Himself said the world would hate His followers, not because they are abrasive, but because they carry a different allegiance. This explains the tension you feel. Yet this is not an accident, and it is certainly not a mistake. God knew exactly what kind of world this would be when He placed you in it. You were not sent here to blend in. You were deployed. You are on a mission to make this world a better place.

If you have ever wondered why obedience feels costly, why righteousness is resisted, or why standing for truth often feels lonely, the answer is simple: this is hostile territory. The world is not designed to affirm God's values. It is designed to challenge them. Yet God did not withdraw you from this environment. He inserted you into it. It is tempting to believe that you are here by chance, born into the wrong era, the wrong culture, the wrong moral climate. That belief is comforting because it removes responsibility. And it is also false. God does nothing by accident. Your generation, your location, your family line, your temperament, and even your struggles were factored into His plan. The book of Acts tells us that God determines the times and places where people live. That means that the time and place where God put you is intentional. You are not misplaced. You are positioned. Like a soldier deployed to a contested zone, you are stationed where resistance is real and the mission matters.

God did not choose you because the environment was easy. He chose you because the environment was difficult and you were suited for it. You are where you are by design, by divine appointment. To be "behind enemy lines" does not mean you are abandoned or outnumbered in the eternal sense. It means you are operating in territory that does not belong to the Kingdom, even though the Kingdom ultimately owns it. This is the tension of the Christian life: you belong to God, but you operate in a world that does not acknowledge His rule. This is why Scripture uses military language like armor, weapons, endurance, vigilance, discipline. These are not metaphors for comfort. They are the language for war and conflict. You are here to represent the King of kings and Lord of lords. You are here to live by a different code than the rest of the world. You are here to advance a different kingdom. Your assignment will never be applauded by the world, but it will always be honored by God.

God did not leave the world in darkness without witnesses to declare His goodness to those deceived by the enemy. He placed His people directly into it to be salt to preserve, light to reveal, ambassadors to represent heaven's interests on earth. You are not called to curse the darkness from a distance; you are called to stand in the middle of it without becoming it. Your presence matters more than you realize. Every act of integrity in a corrupt system, every word of truth spoken in a culture of deception, every decision to obey God when compromise is easier are acts of spiritual warfare. They may be quiet and often unseen, but they are without a doubt eternally significant. As you walk through enemy territory with faith and confidence you can rest assured that God never assigns a mission without provision. If you are behind enemy lines, then you have been equipped accordingly. You have the Spirit of God, the Word of God, the authority of Christ, and the promise that you are never alone.

The goal is not survival - it is faithfulness. Survival focuses on self-preservation, but faithfulness is anchored in obedience, trust, and unwavering commitment to God's will. A faithful life may face hardship, pressure, and loss, yet it remains steadfast when retreat would be easier. In the end, God does not reward those who merely endure, but those who stand firm and finish faithful. The goal is not popularity - it is obedience. Popularity seeks applause from people, but obedience seeks approval from God. When you choose obedience, you may lose favor with the crowd, but you gain alignment with God's will. In the end, obedience always produces lasting fruit, while popularity fades with the opinions of men. The goal is not comfort - it is completion of the assignment. Comfort avoids pressure, but calling requires perseverance, sacrifice, and obedience. True fulfillment comes not from ease, but is found not in avoiding difficulty, but in standing complete before Him, having done all He called us to do.

You are not here to escape the world, but to overcome it by refusing to be shaped by it. You were not saved to retreat into spiritual isolation, nor called to withdraw into a protected bubble where nothing challenges your faith or tests your resolve. The world is constantly pressing, pulling, and persuading people to submit to its evil ways. It has a mold prepared for every person - values to adopt, behaviors to normalize, compromises to justify, and ambitions to chase. Its influence is subtle and relentless. It rarely demands outright rebellion first; instead, it invites small concessions. A softened conviction here. A quiet compromise there. A gradual adjustment until what once shocked you now feels normal, and what once stirred your conscience barely registers at all. But you were never meant to be formed by that mold. To overcome the world does not mean you escape its presence - it means you live in the middle of its systems, cultures, and conflicts without allowing them to define who you are.

You walk through darkness carrying light. You stand in a crooked generation while remaining upright. You engage the world without absorbing its poison. Too many believers confuse holiness with avoidance. They believe spiritual maturity means distancing themselves from anything difficult, messy, or confrontational. But avoidance does not produce strength. Withdrawal does not develop endurance. Comfort does not forge character; it merely preserves what already exists. Character is formed when pressure demands conviction, adversity calls for endurance, and obedience is chosen over ease. You do not grow by hiding from resistance; growth is forged by standing firm within it. Resistance exposes the strength of your convictions and reveals what must be refined, not avoided. When you remain steadfast under pressure, endurance is developed and character is shaped. What once pushed against you ultimately becomes the force that builds you up and makes you strong.

Faith was never meant to be fragile. It was designed to endure pressure, opposition, and the weight of real life. What shatters under hardship was never faith - it was convenience dressed up as belief. True faith grows stronger in the fire, standing firm when everything comfortable is stripped away. The refining work of God often happens not when the pressure is removed, but when the pressure is applied and you choose obedience anyway. The world will test what you truly believe. It will question your values, mock your convictions, and challenge your allegiance. And in those moments you must decide whether you will be shaped by the culture around you or anchored by the truth within you. Overcoming the world begins with the renewal of the mind. The world tries to disciple you every day through social media, conversation, trends, and expectations. It constantly preaches a message: success without sacrifice, pleasure without restraint, identity without responsibility, and freedom without accountability.

If you are not intentional, you will absorb these messages unconsciously and begin living by them instinctively. Spiritual victory is never accidental; it is secured when a believer makes a conscious decision to resist compromise, temptation, and spiritual passivity. Victory comes to those who stand firm, actively opposing the enemy through faith, obedience, and unwavering commitment to God's truth. You overcome by choosing truth over trend. You overcome by submitting your thoughts to God instead of allowing the culture to define reality for you. You overcome by refusing to let noise drown out your inner convictions. You overcome by saying, "This may be popular, but it is not right. This may be accepted, but it is not holy. This may be common, but it is not godly." This kind of resolve is not passive. It requires courage to stand when standing costs you something. It requires humility to obey when obedience makes you look foolish. It requires discipline to remain consistent when compromise would be easier.

Overcoming the world will cost you comfort so don't make the mistake of thinking otherwise. Comfort is built on ease while victory is forged through resistance. The call to rise above the world's systems requires sacrifice, discipline, and a willingness to walk a narrow road when others choose convenience. What you gain in purpose, strength, and eternal reward will far outweigh what you surrender in temporary comfort. The world rewards conformity. It celebrates those who blend in, stay quiet, and go along. But those who refuse to be shaped by it will often feel friction. They will be misunderstood, misrepresented, or marginalized. Yet this resistance is not a sign of failure - it is often evidence of faithfulness. You were not called to be applauded by the world, nor to measure your worth by its approval. You were called to walk in obedience, even when faithfulness goes unnoticed, misunderstood, or opposed. In the end, it is not the applause of people that matters, but the approval of God.

Overcoming the world also means understanding your assignment. You are not here by accident. You were placed in this generation, in this culture, at this time, with intention. God did not miscalculate when He sent you into a broken world - He entrusted you with it. You are here to influence, not to be influenced. To transform, not to conform. To represent heaven while walking on earth. You are the light of the world and light does not negotiate with darkness, nor does it retreat in fear of it. Darkness is not driven away by force, but by the simple, unwavering act of light shining exactly as it was created to shine. When light appears, darkness has no choice but to give way. When you refuse to be shaped by the world, your life becomes a contradiction to it. Your peace confounds anxiety. Your integrity exposes corruption. Your self-control challenges excess. Your faith disrupts fear. And without saying a word, you testify that there is another way to live. This is not arrogance. This is obedience.

The goal is not to escape hardship, temptation, or opposition, because these realities are inevitable in a fallen world. True strength is revealed not by avoidance, but by being steadfast in the face of pressure. Men of character stand in truth when everything around them shifts. They hold fast when others let go and they endure when quitting would be easier. Storms will test what your life is built upon, not merely what you believe. An unshaken life is anchored in conviction, character, and obedience to God. Temptation may knock and opposition may roar, but they do not have authority over a disciplined and submitted heart. The ultimate victory is standing firm, unmoved and faithful, regardless of what surrounds us. You do not overcome the world by overpowering it, but by outlasting it, by remaining faithful when pressure mounts and steady when resistance persists. Victory belongs to those who endure with conviction, trusting that perseverance will ultimately outlive every opposition.

You overcome the world by remaining faithful when pressure demands compromise and steady when chaos insists on reaction. The world is designed to wear you down, not take you out all at once, so victory belongs to those who refuse to quit, refuse to bend, and refuse to let time erode their conviction. Endurance anchored in truth will always outlast force driven by pride. You overcome the world not by overpowering it, but by outlasting it. Empires fall. Trends fade. Popular opinions change. But the man who refuses to be shaped by the world—who anchors their life in God's truth—stands firm long after the noise has passed. You were not placed in this world to merely survive its pressure or reflect its broken patterns. You were called to rise above it - to live transformed, walk in truth, and overcome by purpose, faith, and conviction. You overcome the world by living differently - decisively, courageously, and faithfully - until the world sees not just what you resist, but the God you belong to.

Daniel is a story of a man who was faithful to God. He stood firm in his faith even in enemy territory. He lived for God with strength of spirit, determination, and courage. He learned to lead in a foreign culture even when his own spiritual beliefs weren't popular. He learned to lead by demonstrating qualities like resolve, risk, faith, humility, courage, faithfulness, and integrity. All these qualities were gained from obedience, surrender, and prayer. They came because Daniel was standing firm in the faith. Daniel was one of three leaders directly under Darius, and he shined above the other two because he had an excellent spirit. He had an excellent spirit because he sought the Lord continually. The Bible says he fell on his knees and prayed three times a day. If you want to be strong for God in a culture that hates God, you must "seek the Lord and His strength; seek His presence continually" (1 Chron. 16:11). Daniel was known as a man who stood firm in his faith even when death was looking him in the eye.

We all have spheres of influence. A real man is not defined by the position he holds but by his character. Your character determines who you are and what you do. That's why you can never separate a man's character from his actions. Daniel was a man of character and integrity because he was always standing firm in the faith. He stayed true to his convictions. He wouldn't compromise by eating ritually unclean foods but ate only vegetables. He had pure motives. He didn't take credit for interpreting dreams but glorified God instead. Daniel was known for his honesty. He spoke the truth to authorities regardless of how unpopular his words were. He was a man of discipline. He prayed daily even though it might cost him his life. His integrity was solid. He had no interest in taking bribes or payoffs. He was a loyal friend. He was committed to his friends as he rose through the ranks. Indeed, standing firm in your faith will turn you into a man of character. It will cause you to act like a man.

When you understand why you're here, you'll stop being surprised by resistance. You'll stop interpreting opposition as failure. You'll stop measuring success by comfort or approval. You'll begin to live with clarity and courage. You'll wake up knowing this day matters. You'll walk aware that your choices carry weight. You'll endure hardship knowing it is part of the mission. And most importantly, you'll remember that the darkness around you does not mean God is losing. It means the light you carry is needed. This is why you were chosen and placed in this world for this time. You were sent into the world not to retreat and hide, and definitely not to surrender. You are here to stand, to endure, and to represent the kingdom of

God faithfully right where the battle is fiercest. You are behind enemy lines, yes. But you are exactly where God intended you to be. You were born for such a time as this and it is imperative that you stand firm, be bold, and give it everything you've got. If you don't stand up and fight, who will?

| 10 |

"A MAN OF CHARACTER"

After telling you to be watchful and to stand firm in the faith, 1 Cor. 16:13 next says to "act like men." To act like a man, you should intentionally and vigorously strive to be a man of integrity and character. Becoming a real man is not a matter of age, strength, or appearance. Manhood does not happen by accident. It is forged through choices made in private long before they are displayed in public. A man becomes a man not when life is easy, but when he chooses what is right, even when it costs him. The world has lowered the definition of manhood to dominance and self-gratification. Scripture raises it to something far higher: responsibility, moral courage, faithfulness, and honor. A real man is governed not by impulse, pressure, or convenience, but by conviction. To act like a man is to stand firm in who God has called you to be, rooted in truth, conviction, and unwavering faith. It is a deliberate choice to live with purpose and courage, refusing to be shaped by pressure or fear but by obedience to God's calling.

Real manhood always begins with integrity because a man is only as strong as his commitment to what is right when no one is watching. Integrity anchors his decisions, governs his actions, and keeps his character intact under pressure. Without integrity, strength becomes hollow, but with it, a man becomes trustworthy, grounded, and truly powerful. The Bible consistently teaches that God is far more concerned with who a man is than with what a man does. Actions flow from character. Choices reveal character. Pressure exposes character. And trials refine character. Prov. 11:3 says, "The integrity of the upright guides them, but the unfaithful are destroyed through calculated deception." A man of character is guided by integrity, anchored in truth, and fully submitted to God, allowing his convictions to shape every decision he makes. His life becomes a steady testimony that true strength is found not in appearance or words, but in faithful obedience to what is right.

Prov. 10:9 says, "Whoever walks in integrity walks securely." Integrity means wholeness. A man of character does not live a double life. His words align with his actions. His beliefs align with his behavior. He's the same man in private as he is in public. To walk in integrity is to live with consistency, honesty, and moral uprightness. It implies a life aligned with God's standards, not perfection, but sincerity and wholeness of heart. Integrity removes inner conflict because one's actions match one's values. Integrity is not perfection; it is consistency. It is choosing truth even when lies would be easier. It is keeping promises even when they cost something. It is doing right even when it brings no applause. A Christian man with integrity peaks truthfully, honors commitments, refuses to compromise moral standards, accepts responsibility for his failures, and does not shift blame. Integrity builds trust, and trust is the currency of leadership whether it be in the home, the church, or the workplace.

To walk securely means to live without fear of exposure, collapse, or sudden ruin. A person of integrity does not have to constantly look over their shoulder, manage lies, or defend hidden motives. Their life has stability because it is built on truth rather than deception. Security is a byproduct of integrity. While dishonest gain may seem to offer short-term advantage, it creates vulnerability. Integrity, on the other hand, produces long-term safety - spiritually, relationally, and often practically - because God honors truth and righteousness. A person who chooses integrity builds a life that can bear weight. Truth creates stability, peace of mind, and God-given confidence. Walking right is what allows a person to walk unafraid. Over time, those consistent choices shape you into a man of character, a man who is steady, trustworthy, and rooted in truth rather than convenience. Integrity forges an unshakable inner strength within you and creates a foundation under you that no pressure or opposition can move.

Biblical character does not originate in self-discipline alone - it begins with a holy reverence for God. The fear of the Lord is not terror; it is deep respect, awe, and submission to God's authority. A man who fears the Lord lives with the awareness that God sees, God knows, and God judges rightly. This awareness shapes his decisions even when no one else is present. Prov. 9:10 says, "The fear of the Lord is the beginning of wisdom." A life grounded in the fear of the Lord is built on humility, obedience, and trust, and it is from this foundation that genuine wisdom grows and guides every decision we make. A man of character asks different questions than the world asks. He does not ask, "Will I get caught? Can I get away with this? What do others think? Instead, he asks, "Does this honor God? Is this right? Does this reflect Christ?" The fear of the Lord produces humility, obedience, and moral clarity. Without it, a man may appear disciplined on the outside but lack conviction on the inside.

A Christian man's character is evident not only in what he believes, but in how he treats people, especially those who can offer him nothing in return. Jesus consistently measured righteousness by love, humility, and service. True character is never arrogant, abusive, or domineering. Phil. 2:3 says, "Do nothing out of selfish ambition or vain conceit. Rather, in humility value others above yourselves." True humility is not thinking less of yourself, but choosing to honor others, serve them sincerely, and place their needs ahead of your own. When we live this way, we reflect the heart of Christ and create unity, peace, and genuine love in our relationships. A man of character treats his family with honor, leads with love, not intimidation, shows respect to women, demonstrates patience with children, and extends grace to others while holding firm to truth. Character-driven men understand that authority is a responsibility, not a privilege. Leadership is stewardship, not entitlement.

At its core, Christian character is about Christ-likeness. It's about allowing the life and nature of Jesus to be formed within us. It is revealed not merely in what we profess, but in how we love, forgive, serve, and walk in humility each day. True Christian character reflects Christ to the world through a heart that is wholly and completely surrendered to God. Jesus is the ultimate example of integrity, humility, obedience, courage, and love. A man of character is not trying to impress the world - he is striving to reflect Christ. He leaves a legacy that outlives him. His influence shapes his family, strengthens his church, and honors God. In a generation desperate for real men, God is still calling men to rise - not in arrogance, but in character. The true measure of a man is not determined by the trophies he collects or the milestones he reaches, but by the character he develops along the way. Achievement may impress the world, but integrity, humility, and faith reveal who a man truly becomes.

1 Tim. 3:1-7 lists the godly traits of a man of character, principles that all men should direct their ambitions toward achieving. 1 Tim. 3:1 says, "If a man desires the position of an overseer, he desires an honorable position." An overseer is a leader who oversees people and resources in their family, church, ministry, business, and community. As a man, it is good to aspire to leadership and to intentionally set your heart and mind toward becoming someone others can trust and follow. The word "aspire" means 'to stretch out, to reach after, to grasp something, to yearn for.' True leadership begins on the inside, where character, discipline, humility, and responsibility are cultivated long before authority is ever granted. When a man commits to leading himself well, he positions his life to

positively influence his family, his community, and future generations. An overseer looks over others closely and intently, much like a shepherd might keep very close watch over his sheep.

The overseer is marked by an inward, consuming passion, by an unshakable fire ignited by calling rather than convenience. That inward flame is proven authentic by a disciplined outward pursuit, where daily choices, consistent labor, and faithful endurance give visible form to what burns within. Leadership is not measured by authority exercised over others, but by a willingness to serve them with humility and integrity. True leaders steward the time, talents, and treasures God has graciously entrusted to them for the benefit, growth, and good of those they are called to lead. The world needs more men with character leading and making good decisions. If good men don't do this, bad men will. Paul lists several qualifications and character traits for men who aspire to be leaders and overseers. First, Paul says an overseer "must be blameless" and above reproach, a man of impeccable character (vs. 2). Notice the word "must." This speaks of the absolute necessity of sound, moral behavior.

An overseer must live without disqualifying character flaws or moral defects, conducting himself in a manner that invites trust rather than suspicion. His life should be irreproachable and blameless, marked by integrity that stands up under both scrutiny and pressure. Such a man remains above legitimate criticism because his private conduct consistently aligns with his public calling. This is not describing sinless perfection but that he lives in such a way that he has no controlling character defect. Titus 1:7 says an overseer is "not self-willed, not quick-tempered, not addicted to wine, not violent, not greedy for money." An overseer is called to live above reproach, demonstrating a life where no overt or flagrant sin brings dishonor to the gospel. His conduct must consistently align with the truth he proclaims, because people learn as much from his example as from his words. By walking in integrity, humility, and self-discipline, he provides a clear and trustworthy pattern for others to follow.

A man with character is faithful to his wife (vs. 2). He shows no romantic or sexual interest in other women. He is temperate, self-controlled, and sober-minded, governing his life with discipline rather than impulse. Through self-restraint, he wisely masters every instinct, choosing purpose, clarity, and righteousness over momentary desire. He refrains from any excesses that might cloud his thinking and judgment, submitting to discipline instead of surrendering to indulgence. He exercises control rather than chasing comfort in order to remain clear-minded and focused. By exercising restraint, he protects his ability to discern wisely, act decisively, and honor the responsibility entrusted to him. A true leader understands that authority begins with self-discipline, integrity, and personal accountability. When a man governs himself well, when he masters his own character, decisions, and conduct, he earns the right to influence others and leads not by force, but by example and conviction.

A real man must be prudent which is defined as "acting with or showing care and thought for the future." A prudent man governs his inner life before he ever attempts to govern his outward actions. He disciplines his thoughts, knowing that what he allows into his mind will eventually shape his decisions, words, and behavior. By exercising control over both what he thinks and what he does, he walks in wisdom rather than impulse and lives with purpose and stability. He is well-balanced in both opinion and action, guided by sound reason rather than impulse or pressure. His desires and passions are disciplined and well regulated, allowing him to move with clarity, steadiness, and purpose. He knows his priorities and are devoted to them. Socrates called prudence "the foundation stone of virtue." Dr. Martyn Lloyd-Jones once said, "The great need in the Christian life is for self-discipline." Even Paul said to "work out your own salvation with fear and trembling" (Phil. 2:12).

An overseer must be hospitable, opening both his home and his heart to those he does not yet know. By welcoming strangers with genuine care and kindness, he reflects the love of Christ in practical, visible ways. In doing so, he builds trust, strengthens the body of believers, and demonstrates leadership that serves rather than excludes. He freely offers his time, his resources, and his encouragement to help meet the needs of others, understanding that true strength is expressed through service. He does not give reluctantly or for recognition, but with a willing heart shaped by compassion and responsibility. In doing so, he reflects the character of Christ, proving that generosity is not weakness but a mark of godly maturity. Next,

Paul says an overseer must be "able to teach" (vs. 2). They must be able to teach the Word of God with precision, communicating it clearly and truthfully. An overseer who is not able to teach is like a surgeon who can't use a scalpel or a mechanic who can't use a wrench.

A godly leader demonstrates self-control and strength through gentleness, refusing to be ruled by excess, aggression, or conflict. True maturity is revealed in a steady spirit that values peace, integrity, and devotion to God over money or strife. 1 Tim. 3:3 (GWN) says, "He must not drink excessively or be a violent person, but he must be gentle. He must not be quarrelsome or love money." One of the fruits of the Spirit is self-control, and it is the discipline that governs every other strength a leader possesses. Without self-control, a person may have influence or authority, but they lack the credibility and stability required to lead others well. Paul says an overseer should not be violent, argumentive, or temperamental. The Greek word "plekten" literally means a 'brawler,' someone who is contentious, confrontational, or hot-tempered. In contrast to being violent, an overseer is to be gentle. He is to be a man who is patient and fair-minded under pressure and consistently demonstrates integrity in every situation.

1 Tim. 3:4 (NLT) says, "He must manage his own house well, having children who respect and obey him." A man who seeks the role of an overseer must first demonstrate leadership within his own household. His ability to guide, discipline, and nurture his family with wisdom, consistency, and love reveals his readiness to shepherd others. If he cannot lead his home

with order and godly character, he has not demonstrated the credibility or readiness required to guide and care for others. Titus 1:6 (NLT) says, "He must be faithful to his wife, and his children must be believers who don't have a reputation for being wild or rebellious." A man whose children display unchecked rebellion, or a lack of discipline reveals a failure of leadership at the most foundational level of his responsibility. Leadership begins at home, where character, order, and accountability are first modeled and enforced. If his own children run rampant, how can he claim to be ready to shepherd others with wisdom and faithfulness.

1 Tim. 3:6 (NIV), "He must not be a recent convert, or he may become conceited and fall under the same judgment as the devil." Paul is saying new believers are not prepared to lead other believers. New converts are often filled with genuine passion, but passion alone is not the same as preparation. Spiritual leadership requires maturity, tested character, and a grounded understanding of truth that can only be developed over time. When someone is placed into leadership too quickly, they risk leading from emotion rather than wisdom and conviction. Healthy discipleship allows new believers to grow up, to be rooted and grounded in the faith, and be equipped before they are entrusted with the responsibility of leading others. A believer who is elevated into leadership too quickly may begin to rely on position rather than character, allowing pride to take root before humility is firmly established. Without time to be grounded and tested, that pride can open the door to compromise, ultimately leading to a fall into sin.

All these character traits listed in 1 Tim. 3:1-7 must be evident to those within the kingdom of God and those without. 1 Tim. 3:7 (NIV), "He must also have a good reputation with outsiders, so that he will not fall into disgrace and into the devil's trap." A good reputation is a silent testimony that speaks long after words have faded, revealing the true character of a person's heart. Scripture reminds us that integrity and faithfulness before God and others are more valuable than riches or applause. When we walk uprightly, our reputation becomes a light that honors God and opens doors for His purpose to be fulfilled through our lives. When Jesus walked the earth, He had a good reputation with all the people except for the religious leaders of His day. He was known for His unwavering love, kindness, and generosity, welcoming those society rejected and valuing people others overlooked. He moved with compassion, healing the broken, forgiving sinners, and restoring hope wherever He went.

Paul understood that leadership in the church demands proven character, not merely enthusiasm or gifting. As with new converts, he cautioned that appointing someone prone to moral failure places both the individual and the church at risk, undermining credibility and spiritual stability. He knew that a church leader who carries a bad reputation in the community risks public disgrace, bringing shame not only upon himself but upon the office he represents. Such failure weakens the church's witness and gives opportunity for criticism against the faith itself. Paul warned that this issue was a dangerous trap for both church leaders and the local church, because it subtly shifts trust away from Christ and onto human ability, approval, or control. On the other hand, those who maintain a good reputation both within the church and in the wider community are far more likely to demonstrate the stability, maturity, and proven character necessary to be effectively equipped for trustworthy and enduring leadership.

| 11 |

"A MAN OF VALUE"

A real man is a man of value. In a culture that often measures manhood by status, strength, possessions, or applause, the idea of value has become dangerously distorted. Many men are taught that their worth is tied to what they produce, how much they earn, or how dominant they appear. Yet when these measures fade, so does their sense of identity. A real man is not defined by what he owns or how he is perceived, but by the value he carries within himself and releases into the lives of others. True manhood is anchored in character, not image or bravado, and is shaped by integrity, responsibility, faith, and service. It is revealed in a life that consistently chooses what is right and uses strength to serve others and honor God. It is shaped by integrity, by responsibility that stands firm under pressure, and by faith that trusts God above self. Genuine manhood ultimately expresses itself through service using strength, influence, and ability to lift others rather than exalt oneself.

A man of value understands who he is because his identity is anchored in truth, not opinion, performance, or circumstance. Knowing why he was born gives his life direction and discipline, allowing him to live with purpose and conviction instead of drifting through life by impulse or pressure. His value is not fragile, because it is rooted in something eternal. A man who does not know his value will spend his life trying to prove it. He presents an image and plays a role, quietly hoping others will be convinced of what he himself does not truly believe. But Scripture teaches that value begins with identity. A man's worth is established by his Creator, not by culture. From the beginning, God declared man "very good." This declaration was made before achievements, before titles, and before applause. It was based solely on divine intent. When a man understands that he is created in the image of God, he no longer needs to borrow worth from external sources. He stands secure and confident without being prideful.

One of the clearest indicators of value is conviction. It reveals what a person truly believes, not just what they say. When conviction is present, choices become consistent, courage replaces compromise, and character is proven under pressure. Conviction is what anchors a man, giving him an unshakable foundation when the winds of pressure and compromise begin to blow. It is the inner resolve that keeps him standing firm even when obedience, integrity, and truth demand a personal cost. A real man is not ruled by his moods, urges, or circumstances. He is guided by truth. Men of value do not change their standards to fit the room. They carry their standards into every room they enter. They understand that convenience may offer comfort, but conviction builds legacy. When a man lives by conviction his spoken promise carries the weight of his character. This kind of man may not always be popular, but he is always dependable. People trust him because they know where he stands.

A man of value accepts responsibility instead of avoiding it. He does not blame others for his failures or circumstances. He owns his choices, his words, and his actions. Responsibility is the weight that reveals a man's true strength. It's what presses a man beyond comfort and exposes what he is truly made of. When he shoulders it with courage and integrity, his true strength is no longer claimed - it is revealed for all the world to see. This man understands that leadership begins with self-governance. He manages his time, disciplines his mind, controls his emotions, and directs his energy toward what matters most. He does not run from difficulty; he rises to meet it. Responsibility also extends to how a man treats others. A man of value protects, provides, and serves. He does not use people for personal gain; he invests in them for lasting impact. His presence adds stability, not chaos. Wherever he goes, things are better because his presence brings positive change to everyone and everything he touches.

A man of value serves a purpose greater than himself. He understands that his life is not defined by comfort or self-interest, but by calling and responsibility. He commits his strength, time, and gifts to leaving people better, lifting burdens, and advancing what truly matters. In serving a higher purpose, he finds lasting meaning, legacy, and honor that outlives him. Self-centered men consume; men of value contribute. A real man understands that his life is not just about personal success but about eternal significance. He lives with purpose, knowing he has been entrusted with gifts meant to be given away. A man of value asks, "Who am I helping?" not just "What am I achieving?" He measures success by impact, not applause. He knows that true greatness is found in service, not spotlight. This man uses his strength to lift others, his wisdom to guide others, and his influence to bless others. He leaves rooms fuller than he found them and people stronger than before they met him.

A real man is a man of value, and his character and integrity add worth to every life he touches. A man of value leaves the world better than he found it by building, serving, protecting, and investing in others rather than merely consuming what was given to him. A real man is not remembered for how loud he was, how much he accumulated, or how intimidating he appeared but for the integrity, courage, and faith he lived out every day. His true legacy is measured in the lives he changed, the burdens he lifted, and the hope he ignited in others. His legacy is written in faithfulness, character, and service and when his life is reviewed, it will be said that he left people stronger, better, and closer to their God because he was here. A man of value knows his worth, lives his truth, and walks with God. He stands firm when others waver, gives when others take, and builds when others tear down. In a world desperate for authenticity and strength, this is the man who rises not by force, but by faith.

A man of value is not defined by what he owns, the applause he receives, or the titles he carries. He is defined by how he moves through life especially when life pushes back. A man of value moves victorious through the challenges of life with courage and resilience. He does not shrink under pressure, nor does he collapse when resistance arises. Instead, he stands, adapts, overcomes, and advances. Victory is not the absence of struggle; it is the ability to remain steady, disciplined, and faithful in the midst of it. A man of value understands that success is not one-dimensional. True progress touches every area of life - physical, mental, financial, spiritual, and relational. When one area is neglected, imbalance follows. But when these areas are aligned, a man walks in strength, clarity, and purpose. He becomes a well-balanced man of value - a man who is fit in body, equipped in mind, wise in stewardship, rich in spirit, and aligned in relationships.

Life guarantees challenges and victory requires courage and resilience. Resistance is not a sign that you are on the wrong path; often, it is confirmation that you are moving forward. A man of value does not ask why challenges exist - he prepares himself to face them. Courage is not the absence of fear; it is the decision to move forward in spite of it. Resilience is not toughness alone; it is the ability to recover, refocus, and rise again. Scripture reminds us in Prov.24:16, "The righteous man may fall seven times and rise again." Falling does not disqualify a man but staying down does. A man of value learns from adversity. He grows through difficulty. He refuses to allow hardship to define him or defeat him. Each challenge becomes a training ground, shaping his character and sharpening his resolve. What once tested his limits now forges his strength, teaching him to stand firmer, think clearer, and press forward with unshakable purpose.

A man of value understands that physical fitness is not vanity - it is stewardship. The body is the vessel through which purpose is carried and strength, endurance, and discipline support longevity and effectiveness in every other area of life. Scripture tells us that our bodies are temples of the Holy Spirit (1 Cor. 6:19). This does not demand perfection, but it does require responsibility. A physically fit man honors God by caring for what he has been entrusted with. He develops self-control, consistency, and discipline - qualities that carry over into his spiritual walk, work ethic, and leadership. Physical fitness builds confidence, sharpens focus, and increases resilience. A man who trains his body learns to push through discomfort, delay gratification, and finish what he starts. Each and every disciplined repetition strengthens not only his muscles, but also his resolve to endure, commit, and follow through in every area of life. These are traits of a man who wins in life and overcomes all things that rise against him.

A man of value guards his mind. He is mentally equipped and understands that battles are first won or lost between the ears. Fear, doubt, insecurity, and passivity are mental strongholds that restrict growth, distort perspective, and keep people trapped beneath their true calling. They must be confronted with truth and dismantled through courage and decisive action so faith and purpose can rise unhindered. A sound mind is a trained mind that is intentionally disciplined through truth, practice, and daily renewal to think clearly, choose wisely, and stand firm under pressure. Prov. 23:7 says, "As a man thinks in his heart, so is he." What dominates a man's thoughts will eventually shape his actions and outcomes. A man of value feeds his mind with truth, not noise. He seeks wisdom, not distraction. He chooses clarity over confusion and discipline over fleshly indulgence. He learns to think strategically, respond wisely, and remain emotionally steady even under pressure.

A well-balanced man is financially wise, understanding that money is a tool to be used with purpose, not a master to be served. He directs his resources intentionally, ensuring that his values, faith, and responsibilities always remain in control - not his wealth. A man of value neither chases wealth recklessly nor fears it but governs it with wisdom and unwavering character. He understands stewardship. He lives within his means, plans with foresight, and builds with intention. Financial wisdom produces freedom to provide, to give, to serve, and to pursue purpose without constant strain. Scripture teaches that the borrower is servant to the lender (Prov. 22:7), and a man of value seeks independence through diligence and integrity. Financial progress is not about greed; it is about responsibility. A man of value honors God with his resources, avoids impulsive decisions, and understands the power of consistency over time. He prepares for the future while remaining generous in the present.

Spiritual richness is the source of true strength, the foundation of every other area of life. Without it, strength becomes arrogance, wisdom becomes pride, and success becomes hollow. A man of value is anchored in God. His identity is not fragile because it is rooted in something eternal. A spiritually rich man walks in humility, obedience, and faith. He understands that true power is released not through self-reliance, but through humble alignment with God's will. When his heart and actions are submitted to that divine purpose, his life becomes a conduit for God's authority, wisdom, and enduring strength. Prayer, scripture, and obedience are not religious routines - they are lifelines. When a man is spiritually rich, he has peace in chaos, direction in uncertainty, and hope in adversity. He is not driven by fear of loss because he knows where his strength and provision come from. Matt. 6:33 says, "Seek first the kingdom of God, and His righteousness, and all these things will be added to you."

A spiritually rich man knows that no man succeeds alone. Prov. 27:17 says, "Iron sharpens iron" and this reminds us that we are refined through meaningful, truth-filled interactions with others. When men challenge, encourage, and hold one another accountable in love, character is strengthened and faith is made sharper. A man of value understands the power of healthy relationships. He is aligned relationally with God, with family, with friends, and especially with other men. He chooses integrity over ego. He listens as well as leads. He values loyalty, communication, and trust. Strong relationships provide support, correction, encouragement, and perspective. A man of value does not isolate when challenged. He does not dominate or withdraw. He builds bridges, keeps his word, and treats others with respect. Relational alignment strengthens his leadership by building trust, unity, and influence, and it sustains his legacy by ensuring his impact continues through the people he leads and invests in.

A man of value is not perfect, but he is progressing. He is defined by his unwavering commitment to grow, learn, and move forward with purpose and integrity. The man who is well-balanced is intentional, disciplined, and moves forward with courage. He adapts with resilience. He advances with balance. He is physically fit, mentally equipped, financially wise, spiritually rich, and relationally aligned. This is not accidental living; it is purposeful living. When a man commits to becoming a man of value, victory is no longer a distant hope - it becomes his pattern of life. A man of value is not lost in the sea of life. He is the captain of his own ship and conquers new land wherever he goes. He is not lost in his environment. He is aware of what's happening around him at all times. A man of value is the personification of masculinity, influence, and leadership. Job was a man of high value. Job 1:1 says, "He was blameless, a man of complete integrity. He feared God and stayed away from evil."

If you want to become successful, do not make success your primary pursuit. Instead, make it your aim to become a man of value. When value is present, success becomes inevitable. Many people spend their lives chasing visible rewards: money, recognition, influence, applause, titles, and achievements. They pursue outcomes without first addressing character. They want the fruit without cultivating the root. But success without value is fragile, shallow, and temporary. It may arrive quickly, but it rarely lasts. True, enduring success is always the byproduct of value. It is the effect of consistent habits, disciplined thinking, strong character, and meaningful contribution. When someone focuses only on being successful, they often look for shortcuts, faster routes, easier paths, or external validation. In doing so, they may gain momentary advantage but lose long-term credibility. A person of value, on the other hand, understands that who you are will always determine what you attract.

True value is not measured by what you accumulate, but by what you contribute to the lives and world around you. The impact you make through service, generosity, and purpose becomes the lasting measure of your worth. Value creates demand. Value earns trust. Value solves problems. Value multiplies influence. When you become valuable, people seek you out not because of what you demand, but because of what you bring. Success that is self-centered eventually collapses. But value that is focused outward creates impact that endures. How do you become a person of value? The answer is simple. Refine your God-given gift to the point that the world needs it. When you discover and work on perfecting your gift, your value will go up. People will come looking for you. Prov. 18:16 says, "A man's gift makes room for him and brings him before great men." When those gifts are faithfully developed and humbly offered, God uses them to open opportunities and people you could never reach on your own.

A person's value is based on the principle of rarity. The more rare a thing is, the higher its value. Gold and diamonds are valuable because they are so rare. Rocks and costume jewelry are cheap because they are common. Before you were born, God decided He wanted you to be permanently rare so that you will never lose your value. You are an original and have great value. You are irreplaceable. The most important thing you can do is be yourself. When you focus on becoming a person of value, success no longer needs to be chased. It begins to pursue you. Opportunities open. Doors unlock. Influence expands. Not because you demanded it but because you earned it. Just remember, success will find you when value leads you. If you want a bigger paycheck, become more valuable. If you want greater influence, increase your contribution. Lasting success is built on the depth of your character. Skill may open doors, but integrity, discipline, and faith are what keep them open.

The marketplace rewards value. Relationships reward value. Leadership rewards value. Life rewards value. Do not ask, "How can I become successful?" Ask instead, "How can I become more valuable? What problems can I solve? What burdens can I help lift? What needs can I meet? What value do I bring into a room, a relationship, or an organization?" Because success is not something you seek. It is something that follows a life well-built. Become a person of value and success will have no choice but to follow. The most successful people in any field are not those who demanded the most, but those who served the best. They added clarity where there was confusion. Strength where there was weakness. Order where there was chaos. Hope where there was discouragement. When you consistently invest in making other people better, your influence grows quietly, expands naturally, advances steadily, and develops far beyond what effort alone could ever achieve.

| 12 |

"A MAN WITH PURPOSE"

The foundation of value is character. The world is filled with gifted people who never rise to lasting significance because their character could not support their potential. A man of value is dependable, disciplined, and teachable. He takes responsibility for those under his care and for whatever assignment he's been given from on high. A man of value does what is right even when it is inconvenient or unseen because he knows character is not built in moments of applause but in seasons of obscurity. It is shaped when no one is watching, when no reward is promised, and when quitting would be easy. You cannot add value tomorrow if you refuse to grow today. Growth is not optional for a person of value - it is essential. Stagnation is the enemy of relevance. A person of value is committed to lifelong learning. They read, listen, observe, and refine. They welcome correction rather than resent it. They understand that growth often feels uncomfortable, but stagnation is far more costly.

Growth is the bedrock of value creation. If you stop growing, you stop adding value to your life. If you stop adding value, success stops following. The moment growth stops, contribution stagnates, and your value begins to decline. Success follows motion, and it will not remain where progress has ceased. When you commit to learning, stretching, and improving, you naturally increase what you bring to the table. Growth sharpens your thinking, deepens your wisdom, and increases your capacity to lead, serve, and influence. Anyone can perform well once, but real value is revealed through consistency. The world does not reward occasional excellence - it rewards reliable excellence. People trust those who show up repeatedly. People follow those who remain steady under pressure. People respect those whose behavior aligns with their words. Consistency builds credibility over time, and credibility opens the door to trust, influence, and opportunities that would otherwise remain out of reach.

Ps. 112 describes in great detail what a man of value looks like. Strive daily to act like such a man. Vs. 1 says, "Blessed is the man who fears the Lord, who delights greatly in His commandments." If you want to increase your value both in the sight of God and in the impact of your life, then you must fear God. Stand in awe of Him. Give Him profound reverence. Have a fear of displeasing Him. The fear of God is not terror; it is a holy sense of wonder. It is recognizing who He is and who you are in light of Him. It is standing before His majesty with humility, awareness, and honor. When a man truly fears God, his life gains weight, direction, and substance. To fear God means you take Him seriously. His Word is not optional.

His commands are not suggestions. His presence is not something you casually acknowledge and then ignore. You live with an awareness that God cares deeply about how you live because your character is shaped by who you are before Him when no one else is watching.

True fear of God produces profound reverence. You honor Him in your choices, your speech, your integrity, and your private life. You do not treat sin lightly because you do not treat God lightly. You develop a holy fear of displeasing Him not because He is harsh, but because He is worthy. When a man fears God, his value rises. He becomes trustworthy because his standard is higher than public opinion. He becomes disciplined because he lives before God, not impulses. He becomes dependable because his convictions are anchored, not flexible. He becomes influential because people sense substance, not pretense. Prov. 9:10 says, "The fear of the Lord is the beginning of wisdom." Wisdom adds value. Wisdom stabilizes a life. Wisdom gives a man weight in a world full of noise. If you want to increase your value, do not chase applause. Do not chase status. Do not chase image. Chase reverence and stand in awe of God. When God matters most to you, your life will begin to matter more to others.

The man who fears God delights greatly in His commandments. This verse does not describe a man who merely tolerates God's instructions, but one who finds joy, strength, and direction in them. When a man truly fears God, he no longer sees God's commandments as restrictions. Instead, he understands them as guardrails for blessing. God's Word does not confine him; it frees him. The man who fears the Lord trusts that God's ways are higher, wiser, and more loving than his own. Because of this trust, obedience becomes a pleasure. He delights in God's commandments because he knows they lead to life, peace, and favor. His heart aligns with God's heart, and what God loves, he learns to love as well. Anyone can obey when forced, but delight reveals transformation. Delight means God's Word has moved from being an external rulebook to an internal compass. The man who fears God does not ask, "How little can I do and still be right?" He asks, "How fully can I walk in what pleases the Lord?"

To fear God is to honor Him above all else. To delight in His commandments is to live in joyful agreement with His will. It is the posture of a man who knows that true freedom, fulfillment, and blessing are found in walking closely with the Lord. What grips the heart of a real man is God's Word, God's will, and God's purpose. Joseph did not sin with Potiphar's wife because he feared God and knew He had a purpose for his life. Being a man with purpose will keep you on the right path because you know what God has called you to do. Fear God and you won't veer off course by whatever comes your way. The man who fears God is not easily shaken. He stands firm because his life is built on eternal truth, not shifting opinions or temporary emotions. He has strength, confidence, generosity, and unwavering faith. His delight in God's commandments shapes his decisions, governs his character, and anchors his legacy. His life becomes a testimony that fearing God does not diminish a man - it establishes him.

God's blessings will be on the family of a man of value. Ps. 112:2 says, "His descendants will be mighty on earth; The generation of the upright will be blessed." Notice that the blessings of the next generation is directly tied to the character of the present one. Righteous living does not end with us - it multiplies through generations. Children inherit more than genetics; they inherit examples, values, convictions, and spiritual atmosphere. Wherever you go, people are getting better. Your wife and your children get better because of your value and influence. God is not only concerned with who you are today, but with who your obedience shapes tomorrow. When fathers honor God, they create an environment where faith flourishes. When leaders walk in integrity, they leave behind a blueprint for strength. When believers live righteously, they build a foundation upon which future generations can stand strong. Those who live uprightly will raise a generation that is blessed, strong, and established in the Lord.

Vs.3, "Wealth and riches are in his house, and his righteousness endures forever." The life of obedience and giving honor to God brings God's blessing to your financial affairs. Charles Spurgeon once said, "Uprightness is the road to success. The honest man is the rising man." This verse speaks of wealth and riches, but it anchors those blessings in something far greater: righteousness that endures forever. We are reminded that God is not opposed to blessing His people materially. In fact, scripture openly acknowledges that provision, stability, and abundance can reside in the house of the righteous. God delights in caring for His children. He is a good Father, and good fathers provide. Yet this verse is careful to show us that material wealth is not the centerpiece - it is the byproduct of being a man of purpose, of being a man of upright character The true treasure in this house is righteousness. Wealth may fluctuate, markets may rise and fall, and possessions may fade, but righteousness is eternal.

When a man walks in reverence toward God, his life becomes anchored in values that outlast any temporary success. His integrity stands when money fails. His character remains when circumstances change. Notice also that the verse connects wealth to stewardship, not selfishness. "In his house" implies order, responsibility, and purpose. God entrusts resources to those who will manage them wisely and use them to bless others. The righteous man understands that prosperity is not merely for consumption, but for contribution. It's for supporting his family, advancing God's work, and lifting those in need. Ps.112:3 calls for us to reframe our understanding of success. True prosperity is not measured only by what fills our bank accounts, but by what fills our hearts and governs our lives. When a life of righteousness is established, blessing has a firm foundation. When righteousness endures, the impact of our lives extends far beyond our years. That's what being a man with purpose is all about.

Vs. 4, "Unto the upright there arises light in the darkness." Notice that darkness is already present. The upright are not spared trials, confusion, or hardship. What distinguishes them is not the absence of trouble, but the certainty of divine illumination in the midst of it. God does not always remove the darkness, but He causes light to rise inside it. In fact, God Himself is the light which arises in darkness for those who are sincere in their dealings with Him. The verse connects light with uprightness. Uprightness does not mean perfection; it means alignment. It means walking with integrity, humility, and reverence for God. When a person chooses obedience over compromise and trust over fear, they position themselves for God's light to break through. Darkness may linger through the night, but dawn is inevitable. God's promise to the upright is not a temporary flicker, but a steady increase of illumination. What begins as a glimmer becomes clarity. What starts as reassurance becomes confidence.

Vs. 4 continues, "He is gracious, and full of compassion, and righteous." The light received from God shines through the man of value into the life of others. To be gracious is to reflect the generosity of God's heart. Grace flows from him toward his family, toward strangers, toward those who may not deserve it. Grace is evidence that God's presence governs a life more than circumstances do. Everything comes alive when you walk into a room. The mood changes for the better because you are standing in their midst. Compassion is grace in motion. In a dark world that grows colder by the day, compassion becomes a beacon - proof that God is still at work through yielded hearts. Righteousness anchors the soul. The righteous man does what is right even when it is costly, unseen, or unpopular. His integrity produces stability, and that stability allows God's light to shine steadily through him. When a man with purpose walks through darkness, he does not merely survive it - he illuminates it.

Vs. 5, "A good man deals graciously and lends; He will guide his affairs with discretion." This verse gives us a clear, practical picture of what a man with purpose looks like in the eyes of God. It is not merely a description of character, but a blueprint for living a stable, influential, and God-honoring life. Grace reveals confidence in God. When a man is secure in the Lord, he does not need to dominate others or prove himself. He can afford to be gentle, because he trusts God to defend, promote, and establish him. The willingness to lend speaks of generosity, but it also speaks of stewardship. This man lives in such a way that he has something to give. He manages his life responsibly, honors God with his resources, and keeps his heart open to the needs of others. Lending in Scripture is not reckless giving - it is purposeful generosity. It reflects a man who understands that what he has is a trust from God, not merely personal possession. He gives without manipulation and helps without control.

A man of value shares with others the generosity God has granted to him. With love and kindness, God sees the quiet tears of the poor widow and the single mother who struggles to pay her bills, and He is not indifferent to their need. In His perfect timing, He provides help, hope, and relief - often through compassionate hearts willing to act on His behalf. A man with purpose will make right choices because he's been blessed with divine wisdom that flows from his godly character. He is recognized by how he treats people, how he handles resources, and how he navigates decisions. Grace shapes his relationships. Generosity marks his influence, leaving a trail of lives strengthened and burdens lifted because he chose to give. Wisdom secures his future, guiding his steps with discernment, stability, and lasting purpose. This is the kind of life that honors God and blesses others - a life guided not by impulse or selfish ambition, but by grace, generosity, and godly discretion.

Vs. 6, "Surely he will never be shaken; The righteous will be in everlasting remembrance." Because of his character and wisdom, the man who fears God will be firmly established. Lives rooted in God are never uprooted. The righteous are not immune to storms, but they are unshaken by them. Their confidence is not rooted in wealth, position, or approval, but in the unchanging character of God. When fear rises, they stand firm. When the world trembles, they remain steady. Their footing is secure because it rests on obedience, trust, and reverence for the Lord. God does not forget faithfulness. The righteous may never chase applause, but heaven takes notice. Their lives leave an imprint that outlives them - on families, on communities, and in the purposes of God. Long after their voice grows silent, the testimony of their walk with God continues to speak. Charles Spurgeon said, "The righteous are worth remembering, and God Himself takes charge of their memorials."

Everlasting remembrance is not about fame; it is about impact. It is the legacy of integrity, consistency, and quiet courage. It is the memory of someone who stood for what was right when it was costly, who walked with God when it was inconvenient, and who trusted Him when it required faith. A life lived for God is never wasted. It is steady, secure, and significant. The righteous may pass from this world, but their influence does not fade, because God Himself remembers their lives of faith and obedience. Though their voice may fall silent on earth, their testimony continues to speak through the work God accomplished in and through them. What the Lord remembers is not subject to time, decay, or forgetfulness. Heaven preserves the impact of every righteous deed, prayer, and sacrifice. What God remembers endures forever, leaving an eternal imprint that no grave can erase. Live anchored. Walk uprightly. Your life, grounded in God, will not be shaken and it will be remembered.

Vs. 7, "He will not be afraid of evil tidings. His heart is steadfast, trusting in the Lord." He who trusts in the Lord stands unshaken when troubling news arises, because his confidence is anchored in God, not circumstances. Evil tidings come to everybody yet the man who fears the Lord will not be afraid. Ps. 23:4 says, "Though I walk through the valley of the shadow of death, I will fear no evil for You are with me." A man of value is stable and emotionally strong. He is not easily moved. His heart is propped up by the strength of his Lord. He is neither fickle nor is he cowardly. When he is undecided as to his course, he is still fixed in his heart. He has the ability to recognize, understand, and manage his emotions. A man who controls his emotions leads himself with strength and clarity rather than being driven by impulse. He controls his emotions; they don't control him. Mastery over emotions produces stability, discernment, and a quiet authority that increases a man's true value.

Vs. 8, "His heart is established; He will not be afraid until he sees his desire upon his enemies." A man with purpose has confidence in God's justice. This is not about personal vengeance, but about trusting God to bring truth to light and to overturn what rises against righteousness. When your heart is anchored in the Lord, fear is replaced with faith, and you can stand steady knowing that God will finish what He has started. This is why the heart of a man of value is steadfast and unmovable. He will not fear while he looks on his adversaries. When a man's heart is fixed on the Lord, fear loses its authority because his confidence is no longer rooted in circumstances but in God's faithfulness. He does not rush to panic or revenge; he stands firm, trusting that God will bring justice in His time, allowing him to remain steady until victory is revealed and opposition is overcome. Faith produces patience, and patience produces peace, allowing the believer to stand calmly while God works behind the scenes.

The profile of a man of value who fears the Lord is truly remarkable. Vs. 9 says, "He has dispersed abroad, he has given to the poor. His righteousness endures forever. His horn will be exalted with honor." Horns are weapons used for fighting off predators. It is a symbol for strength, honor, and dignity. It comes from the image of a bull lifting up its horns after winning a battle. A man of value will rise to influence only through his own worth, and not by extortion or flattery. He is a wise man. He guides his affairs with discretion. He is a strong man and is not afraid of evil tidings. He is a prosperous man who makes a home for his family and descendants. He leaves an inheritance for his children's children (Prov. 13:22). He is a loving and kind man. He is gracious and full of compassion. He is a helping man. He deals graciously and lends. With prudence and discretion, he sows financial seeds in good ground so as to produce the most bountiful harvest. Wise living is always characterized by lasting success.

| 13 |

"A GOOD REPUTATION"

It was Albert Einstein who said, "Try not to become a person of success, but rather try to become a person of value." He knew that value is directly connected to success. The more valuable you are, the more successful you will be. Success follows value because the marketplace rewards those who consistently solve problems, add insight, and produce results. The more skills you develop, the more character you build, and the more value you bring to others, the greater your opportunities become. Increase your value, and success will pursue you rather than the other way around. At the same time, value is also connected to influence. When your value grows, your influence naturally increases in the lives of other people. As your character, competence, and integrity develop, others begin to trust your voice and follow your example. The more you invest in becoming better, the more power you have to make a meaningful difference in the lives of those around you.

Men with the most influence are those who discover and pursue their purpose and are driven by their passions. Purpose ignites passion which keeps you motivated, inspired, and focused. You must also embrace a lifelong pursuit of personal development. Take time to refine yourself in every area of life because intentional growth is what transforms potential into lasting purpose. Be original. Be unique. Be unapologetically authentic. Imitation may blend in, but originality stands out and leaves a lasting impact. Be you and boldly live as the person God uniquely created you to be because no one else can fulfill that calling but you. Your value depends on the value you offer others. Choose a problem you can solve for people. Think of what you can do to help make the lives of other people better. The more problems you help solve, the more value you bring into the lives of others. When people see that you consistently make their burdens lighter, your impact and leadership grow.

Pursue excellence. Becoming a person of value is not so much about what you do, but about the excellence and integrity you bring to it. True value is revealed when you give your best effort, even in the smallest and unseen tasks. When you consistently do things well, your character speaks louder than your accomplishments. If it's worth doing, it's worth doing well because excellence honors both the task and the one who undertakes it. Going beyond the usual separates the ordinary from the unforgettable and turns effort into impact. Add a touch of class in all you do, and let your work quietly speak of discipline, purpose, and pride. Also, encourage and inspire others wherever you go, because your words and actions can awaken potential they may not yet see in themselves. Share your knowledge and skills with others. Empower them to be a greater version of themselves. Look for ways to help people become all they can be, and in doing so, you elevate both their future and your own.

Your true value and influence are measured by how many lives are improved because of your presence. When you choose to serve, encourage, and uplift others, your impact multiplies far beyond what you can see. Radiate confidence wherever you go. Carry yourself with purpose, clarity, and conviction. Know what you want, and with bold faith and unwavering confidence, go after it without hesitation. When you walk in genuine self-confidence, people are naturally drawn to your presence and your purpose. Confidence opens hearts and minds, making others receptive to your influence and leadership. Be a man of integrity. Your word and your actions must align even when no one is watching. True value and lasting influence are built when people can trust you, because confidence is earned through consistency, honesty, and character. Live by godly values and uphold sound moral principles. Be sincere and real. Do the right thing at all times and in all circumstances whether it's convenient or not.

When you obey God's command to act like a man, you will create for yourself a good reputation. The word "reputation" refers to how much respect or admiration someone receives based on their character and past behavior. Scripture consistently teaches that a man's reputation matters. Prov. 22:1 says, "A good name is more desirable than great riches; to be esteemed is better than silver and gold." The NLT says, "Choose a good reputation over great riches; being held in high esteem is better than silver or gold." AMP, "A good name earned by honorable behavior, godly wisdom, moral courage, and personal integrity is more desirable than great riches." When God calls you to act like a man, He is not appealing to cultural stereotypes or shallow displays of toughness. He is calling you to spiritual maturity, moral courage, responsibility, and steadfast faith. Obedience to that command produces something enduring: a reputation that heaven honors and people trust.

A good reputation comes when you have a lifestyle of protecting and promoting the well-being of others. In a world that often equates reputation with popularity, image, or public applause, God defines reputation differently. A godly reputation is not built through self-promotion, loud claims, or outward strength. It is formed through obedience - quiet, consistent, costly obedience to the commands of God. Challenge yourself to live with integrity, excellence, and consistency so that your reputation precedes you wherever you go. The word "precede" means 'to come before' and "reputation" means 'the beliefs or opinions held about someone.' If your reputation precedes you, it means people have heard things about you before they actually see you. Someone may say, "I've never met you, but I already know all about you based on the opinions of other people I've heard." Let your reputation open doors, build trust, and reflect the values you stand for wherever you go.

To "act like a man" in biblical terms means to live with alertness, conviction, strength of character, and submission to God's authority. This command is not optional. It is not reserved for certain seasons of life or certain personality types.

It is a call to every man who desires to walk in the fullness of God's purpose. Obedience to this command requires action. It demands that a man rise above passivity, fear, and compromise. It challenges him to lead when it would be easier to retreat, to stand when it would be safer to blend in, and to obey God even when obedience comes at a cost. True manhood begins on the inside. A man who obeys God develops spiritual muscle long before anyone notices his outward success. Each act of obedience strengthens his resolve and sharpens his discernment. Over time, this produces a man who is not easily shaken by pressure, criticism, or adversity. Obedience trains a man to respond rather than react. Instead of being driven by emotion or impulse, he is governed by truth.

This inner strength becomes evident in how he handles conflict, temptation, responsibility, and hardship. People may not know all the choices he has made in private, but they will see the fruit of those choices in his life. Reputation cannot be demanded; it must be earned. A man who obeys God consistently will eventually be known for reliability, integrity, and courage. His words carry weight because his life backs them up. His presence brings stability because people know where he stands. Biblical examples confirm this truth. Joseph's obedience in private built a reputation that eventually positioned him for public leadership. David's faithfulness in obscurity prepared him for authority in the kingdom. Even Jesus "grew in wisdom and stature, and in favor with God and man" (Luke 2:52). A good reputation does not mean a man will be universally liked. Obedience to God will sometimes provoke opposition. However, even critics are forced to acknowledge consistency, honesty, and moral strength over time.

Obedience always precedes influence. It is the quiet proving ground where God shapes the heart before He entrusts it with impact. When you faithfully submit to His will in the unseen places, He releases influence in His timing, knowing your life will point others to Him and not to yourself. Obedience is not limited to dramatic moments. It is expressed in daily decisions like embracing discipline rather than giving in to indulgence, choosing truth over convenience, responsibility over avoidance, faith over fear, and service over selfishness. A man who acts like a man keeps his word, honors his commitments, protects what God has entrusted to him, and takes responsibility for his actions. He does not shift blame or hide behind excuses. He understands that leadership begins with personal accountability. These choices shape how a man is known in his home, workplace, church, and community. Over time, obedience becomes a pattern, and that pattern becomes a reputation.

Reputation is not only about how a man is known today - it is about what he leaves behind. A godly reputation influences families, strengthens communities, and inspires future generations. When a man obeys God's command to act like a man, he shows the world that real manhood is anchored in faith, shaped by obedience, and proven through character. Every man is building a reputation, whether intentionally or unintentionally. The question is not if a reputation will be formed, but what kind. Obedience to God's command to act like a man lays a solid foundation that cannot be shaken by time, circumstance, or opinion. A good reputation is not the result of perfection, but of faithfulness. When a man chooses obedience day after day, God shapes his character, strengthens his resolve, and establishes his name. In doing so, that man discovers a powerful truth that when you act like a man according to God's design, you do not just live well, you leave a legacy that matters.

To act like a man, you must spend quality time with God and be led by the Holy Spirit throughout the day. When you're led by the Spirit, you'll be able to control your actions, and actions, over time, is what earns you your reputation. The Holy Spirit was never given merely to make us emotional or expressive; He was given to make us obedient, disciplined, and transformed. When you are truly led by the Spirit, your life begins to reflect restraint, wisdom, and consistency. The Spirit does not drive us into chaos; He leads us into order. He does not excuse reckless behavior; He empowers self-control. Scripture is clear when it says, "For God has not given us a spirit of fear, but of power, love, and a sound mind" (2 Tim. 1:7). A sound mind grounded in truth and wisdom produces sound decisions that guide your actions with clarity and purpose. Over time, these sound decisions when made consistently will form a solid reputation forged through trust, integrity, and a legacy that endures.

Being Spirit-led means you no longer live at the mercy of impulses, emotions, or circumstances. You don't react - you respond. You don't lash out - you listen. You don't give in - you stand firm. The Spirit puts a governor on your life.

He teaches you when to speak and when to be silent, when to move and when to wait, when to confront and when to walk away. This inner leadership shapes your outward behavior. Too many people want the appearance of spirituality without the discipline of spirituality. But the Holy Spirit is not impressed with appearances - He is committed to transformation. He works from the inside out, shaping your thoughts, guiding your choices, and correcting your actions over time. And that word "time" matters because reputation is never built overnight. Reputation is the long-term result of repeated actions, shaped day by day through what you choose to do. It isn't built by a single statement, but by consistent behavior that proves who you truly are.

Anyone can have a good moment, but character is proven in patterns. When the Spirit leads you day after day, your actions begin to line up with God's nature. You become dependable, trustworthy, and steady. People may not know every detail of your faith, but they will recognize your integrity. The fruit of the Spirit is not about church performance - it's about life control. Love controls how you treat others. Joy controls how you respond to hardship. Peace controls how you handle conflict. Patience controls your temper. Kindness controls your words. Faithfulness controls your commitments. Gentleness controls your strength. And self-control governs it all. These fruits show up in action, not theory. Over time, those actions speak louder than any testimony. People are watching what you say and do and when they see your consistency - when they see you handle pressure without compromise, success without pride, and correction without rebellion - you earn credibility. That credibility is your reputation.

A Spirit-led person understands that every choice is a seed. What you plant today, you will harvest tomorrow. If you sow discipline, you reap trust. If you sow humility, you reap honor. If you sow obedience, you reap favor. The Holy Spirit helps you sow wisely, even when your flesh wants immediate gratification. He teaches you not to live for the moment but to think long-term because God always builds for the future. What looks like delay to us is often development in His hands. While we focus on the present moment, God is already working toward what is next. God has never been a short-term thinker. From the very beginning, He built with generations in mind. Every promise He spoke, every covenant He established, and every instruction He gave was aimed not just at immediate results, but at lasting impact. The Holy Spirit teaches us to think beyond convenience and emotion. He pulls our eyes off what feels good now and lifts them toward what will matter later.

God always builds for what is coming. He shapes character before He releases blessing. He prepares hearts before He opens doors. He strengthens roots before He allows growth. That is why the Spirit often leads us into seasons of discipline, patience, and unseen preparation. What feels slow is often strategic. What feels hidden is often foundational. The Holy Spirit reminds us that seeds are never planted for immediate harvest. They are planted with expectation. God thinks in terms of legacy, of families restored, faith passed down, and lives influenced long after we are gone. When the Spirit renews your mind, He teaches you to invest, not consume; to prepare, not rush; to obey, not demand. Walking with the Holy Spirit means learning to delay gratification in order to fulfill divine purpose. It means trusting that God is building something greater than the moment you are standing in. What God is doing in you today is not just for today. It is preparation for what is ahead.

The Spirit trains us to live wisely, love deeply, and choose obedience because God is always constructing a future that outlives us. A good reputation is not about being perfect; it's about being governed. Governed by truth. Governed by conviction. Governed by the Spirit of God. People trust those who are governed because they are predictable in the best way - they can be counted on to do what is right even when it's hard. When you are led by the Spirit, you stop needing to defend yourself. Your actions defend you. You stop needing to announce who you are, because your life confirms it. The Spirit teaches you that silence, faithfulness, and obedience will speak louder than self-promotion ever could. In the end, God is less concerned with how spiritual you sound and more concerned with how faithfully you walk. The Spirit leads you not just to heaven, but to maturity. And as you walk in that leadership day by day, your actions will form a reputation that reflects Christ.

To earn a good reputation, you must demonstrate respect for other people. Genuinely care for them and show it. Be real. Talk authentically. Use simple and understandable language. Listen sincerely to the things that matter most to them. Let people know where you stand. Generate transparency. Tell the truth in a way that can be confirmed. Always practice full disclosure. Correct offenses. Apologize quickly. Make amends where possible. Be trustworthy. Give credit generously. Talk about people as if they were present. Deliver results. Continuously improve toward mastery. Learn to say "thank you" as often as possible. Practice accountability. Take responsibility for your words and actions. Listen to people. Don't assume you know what matters most to others. Keep commitments. Don't break confidences. Extend trust abundantly to those who have earned it. It's very inspiring when you act like a man. It's what attracts opportunities for you to influence others in a positive way.

Your reputation is a precious commodity. If protected and cultivated, it can assure success. Warren Buffet said, "It takes twenty years to build a reputation and five minutes to ruin it. If you think about that, you'll do things differently." Building a strong, positive reputation takes diligent effort. Maintaining such a reputation takes as much effort if not more. It is critical that you seize each and every opportunity to build and maintain a strong, godly reputation. Reputation is what people expect you to do next. It's their expectation of the quality and character of the next thing you say and do. The man people trust most is the one who does what he says he's going to do in the time frame promised. How do you build a good reputation? Go above and beyond what is expected. Cultivate a positive outlook. Care about and help others. Find solutions to problems. Do what you say you will do. Are you honest? Dependable? Are you a man of integrity? These things impact how much trust others place in you.

| 14 |

"A FORCE FOR GOOD"

You need to build a good reputation wherever you go. When your name is mentioned, how do people respond? People may know you at church, but what behavior are you known for out in the world? It's easy to be recognized where you worship, to lift hands during worship, to say "amen" at the right time, to quote scripture among believers. But the true measure of faith is not found in the pew - it's revealed in public. What are you known for outside the sanctuary? Are you known for patience when others are difficult? For integrity when no one is watching? For kindness when there's nothing to gain? For humility when pride would be easier? Being in church reveals what you believe but being out in the world reveals what you practice. Jesus never said the world would recognize us by our church attendance, our titles, or our religious language. He said they would know us by our fruit. Your words may inspire on Sunday, but it is your daily actions that truly reveal what you believe and who you serve.

The world may never open your Bible, but it watches how you live every day. Your actions, attitudes, and words preach a message louder than any verse you can quote. Live in such a way that when people read your life, they see Christ clearly written there. How you treat people who can't benefit you, how you respond under pressure, how you speak when you're frustrated, how you live when faith costs you something - that is the sermon the world hears. If someone followed you for a week and heard your conversations and saw your actions and took notice of the choices you made, would they see Christ reflected? Being known at church is good, but it's only the beginning of your witness. The true measure of faith is not who recognizes you in the pews, but who sees Christ in you in everyday life. When your walk reflects Jesus everywhere you go, your life becomes the message the world cannot ignore because the strongest testimony is not what you claim on Sunday - it's who you are on Monday.

Live in such a way that when people speak your name, they don't just think, "They go to church," but instead say, "There's something different about them." How you act shapes how the world perceives you, and perception often determines the opportunities you are given or denied. A man who carries himself with integrity, discipline, and confidence earns trust, respect, and influence over time. If you want lasting success, align your actions with the man you want God and others to see you as. Your reputation speaks long before you ever open your mouth to lead. People decide whether to trust your direction based on the consistency, integrity, and character they have already observed in your life. If your walk aligns with your words, others will willingly follow where you are headed. Without a doubt, your reputation precedes you. This means people will hear about you before they meet you. The good news is that when you act like a man, your reputation will speak for itself.

1 Kings 10:1 tells how the queen of Sheba "heard about the fame of Solomon and his relationship to the Lord." Solomon was known far and wide for his wisdom, integrity, and close walk with God, and his reputation drew nations to hear him. His life reminds us that a godly reputation is built not just on words, but on daily obedience and reverence for the Lord. When people speak your name, do they also think of your faith, your character, and your devotion to God? Have others heard through your life as much as your lips about your relationship with the Lord? The queen said to Solomon, "The report I heard in my own country about your achievements and your wisdom is true. Your wisdom and prosperity exceed the fame of which I heard" (vs. 6,7). If you want a good reputation like Solomon had, then don't keep silent about the God you serve. Boldly proclaim that you are a child of the living God. Show the world the type of man you are by living your faith with integrity, courage, and consistency.

Having value and a good reputation speaks volumes about the influence a real man can exercise for the good of society. A man of value is not measured merely by his possessions, position, or popularity, but by the weight of his character and the consistency of his conduct. His reputation is built quietly over time through integrity, faithfulness, and the willingness to do what is right even when it is costly or unseen. Such a man understands that his name is a trust, and he guards it carefully because he knows it represents who he truly is when no one is watching. A good reputation gives a man influence beyond words. People listen to him not because he demands attention, but because his life has earned credibility. His actions align with his convictions, and that alignment creates trust. A real man uses his reputation to lift others up, not to elevate himself. He understands that his choices affect more than just his own life; they shape the atmosphere around him and set an example for the next generation.

Ultimately, a man of value recognizes that his reputation is a reflection of his inner life. It is formed by daily decisions, quiet obedience, and a steadfast commitment to righteousness. Such a man leaves a lasting impact, not because he sought recognition, but because he lived with purpose and integrity. His influence becomes a force for good in society, proving that when a man knows his value and guards his reputation, he becomes a pillar others can stand upon and a light that points the way forward. We are here to bring light in the midst of darkness, standing as beacons of hope where fear and despair try to reign. We bring order in the midst of chaos by living with purpose, truth, and unwavering faith. When we walk in that calling, darkness retreats and lives are transformed. When you act like a man you bring life into places that seem dead and broken. Your strength becomes a beacon of hope, cutting through despair and reminding others that renewal is still possible.

Men with a good reputation are men of integrity, because reputation is not built by words alone but by consistent, righteous living. Integrity means the same man shows up in public and in private, when eyes are watching and when no one is looking. His character is not shaped by convenience or pressure, but by conviction. He does not bend his values to fit the moment; he stands firm even when it costs him something. A man of integrity understands that talk is cheap, but actions are costly and that is where true character is proven. Many can speak convincingly about honor, faith, responsibility, and courage, but only a few are willing to live those principles when it requires sacrifice. Men with a good reputation are not perfect, but they are consistent. When they fall, they own it. When they fail, they repent, correct course, and keep moving forward. They do not hide behind excuses or blame others for their shortcomings; instead, they take full responsibility and rise stronger through accountability.

Walking the walk means doing the right thing when it would be easier to do the wrong thing. It means keeping your word even when breaking it would benefit you. It means showing up on time, fulfilling your responsibilities, honoring commitments, and treating people with respect regardless of what you can gain from them. Integrity shows up in how a man handles his money, his relationships, his work, and his faith. It is revealed in the small, unseen decisions that eventually shape a visible life. A good reputation is not something a man demands; it is something others freely give because they have watched his life over time. Trust is earned through repeated demonstrations of faithfulness. When a man says he will do something - and then does it - his words begin to carry weight. People listen to him not because he is loud, but because he is reliable. His presence anchors our hearts in peace, replacing chaos with stability and confusion with quiet confidence.

Men of integrity understand that leadership begins with self-discipline. Before they can influence others, they must govern themselves. They refuse to live double lives, saying one thing while doing another. Instead, their speech and their behavior align. Their beliefs shape their actions, and their actions reinforce their beliefs. This alignment is what gives them credibility and authority. Ultimately, a man with a good reputation leaves a lasting impact because his life tells the same story his mouth does. His walk confirms his talk. His example inspires others to rise higher, live better, and pursue integrity for themselves. In a world full of empty words and broken promises, men who walk the walk stand out and their integrity becomes their legacy. When you do all that, you will learn very quickly that your reputation will travel near and far. Integrity, consistency, and faith-filled action speak louder than words, carrying your name into places you may never step but your influence will reach.

The queen of Sheba lived in a foreign country, yet she heard about the reputation and fame of Solomon. You can't keep to yourself the things you say and do. People will hear about it, sometimes even in foreign countries. Every word you speak and every action you take carries weight. You may think what you do is hidden, confined to a moment, a room, or a small circle but nothing truly stays private for long. Life has a way of echoing truth far beyond where it was first spoken. Scripture reminds us that "what is whispered in the ear will be proclaimed from the housetops" (Matt. 10:27). Our lives are always preaching a message, whether we intend them to or not. The way you treat people, the choices you make when no one is watching, and the words you release in casual conversation all become seeds. Those seeds travel. Faithfulness opens doors you never knocked on. Sometimes they reach places you never imagined - across cities, across generations, and yes, even into foreign lands.

This is why integrity matters. This is why God calls us to live wisely, speak carefully, and walk humbly. You may never meet the people influenced by your obedience - or affected by your disobedience - but they exist. Your life is a testimony on the move, speaking louder through daily obedience than through words alone. As you walk in faith, every step becomes evidence that God is real, active, and transforming lives. So let your words be seasoned with grace. Let your actions reflect Christ. Live in such a way that if your story travels farther than you ever do, it still honors God. Because whether you like it or not, what you say and do will be heard - sometimes in places you never planned to reach. News travels fast, and word spreads quickly about how you live and lead. A good reputation is not built overnight but through consistent character and integrity. Every choice you make becomes part of the story others tell about you. In time, if you remain faithful and true, the whole world will hear about it.

The queen of Sheba came to where Solomon was. Like a magnet, his reputation drew her in. A good reputation will draw people in; a bad reputation will push them away. Your reputation speaks long before your mouth ever opens. It introduces you when you are not in the room. It tells others what they can expect from you whether you will be a blessing or a burden. When your life reflects faith, kindness, faithfulness, and self-control, people are drawn to you because they know you're trustworthy. They feel safe. They listen. They lean in. Your character opens doors that talent never could. But a bad reputation does the opposite. It repels rather than attracts. It builds walls instead of bridges. Even truth spoken by someone with a damaged reputation often goes unheard because trust has been broken. So guard your name and protect your witness. As believers, the way we speak, treat others, keep our word, and handle conflict all preach a message, whether we intend to or not.

Live in such a way that when people encounter you, they encounter integrity, grace, and faith in action. A good reputation doesn't just draw people to you; it draws them closer to God, because your life becomes a visible reflection of His character. When integrity, love, and faith guide your actions, others are inspired to seek the Source behind the light they see in you. You can come to a place where people can see your reputation. They'll see the physical evidence of the things you have done for the Lord. They'll see physical evidence of your obedience, integrity, and accountability. The queen of Sheba saw the glorious splendor of Solomon's kingdom and was truly amazed (vs. 4-8). A good reputation impacts the lives of other people.

The queen was overwhelmed by what she saw. Her life was impacted. She was inspired by all the glorious things she saw. Act like a man and have a positive impact on the lives of those around you. Go all out and help make the lives of other people better.

Building a good reputation first and foremost begins with your relationship with the Lord. Build a strong relationship with the Lord and you will build a good reputation. The queen of Sheba heard of Solomon's reputation with the Lord, and she came to see him. Matt. 6:33 says to "seek first the kingdom of God and His righteousness." Put God first and you'll have a good reputation. Zech. 4:6 says, "Not by might nor by power, but by My Spirit says the Lord." Also, you build a good reputation by walking in wisdom. Wisdom is knowing how to apply the knowledge you have. The queen of Sheba saw all the wisdom of Solomon and the palace he had built (vs. 4). Solomon's wisdom was demonstrated by the palace he built. He applied the knowledge he had and built a glorious palace. The queen looked around and saw the work of his wisdom. Get knowledge and apply it correctly. Knowledge becomes wisdom when it is rightly applied. Understanding alone informs, but correct application transforms.

Showing hospitality to others opens doors to trust, respect, and genuine connection. When people feel welcomed and valued through your kindness, your character speaks louder than your words. Over time, consistent hospitality builds a good and lasting reputation that reflects both integrity and love for others. Solomon prepared a special meal for his quest, and she was overwhelmed by the elegance of it all (vs.5). Always treat people with love and respect, choosing generosity over selfishness in every situation. When you put the needs of others above your own, you reflect true character and create a lasting impact that reaches far beyond yourself. Be like the Good Samaritan who sacrificed his time and resources to help a man beaten by robbers when others chose to walk away. True faith is revealed not in passing by, but in stepping in and loving when it costs you something. Prov. 3:27 says, "Do not withhold good from those to whom it is due, when it is in the power of your hand to do so."

Never forget it is God you represent. The Message Bible says, "Your hand is God's hand for that person." Be generous with your kindness and your love, freely giving of your time, your talents, and your treasures. When you pour yourself out for others, you reflect the heart of God and create ripples of blessing that return far greater than what you gave. Give generously, and you will reap a good reputation that speaks louder than words. Acts of kindness plant seeds of honor that take root in the hearts of others. As generosity continues, that reputation will grow and grow and grow. Prov. 11:24 (MSG), "The world of the generous gets larger and larger, the world of the stingy gets smaller and smaller." If you want to grow your reputation, be a generous giver, because generosity leaves a lasting imprint on the hearts of others. People may forget what you said or did, but they never forget how you made them feel. When you give freely, you build trust, honor, and a legacy that speaks long after you're gone.

The queen of Sheba said, "How happy your people must be! How happy your officials who continually stand before you and hear your wisdom" (vs. 8). The people working for Solomon were happy because they were treated well. When the queen saw the seating of Solomon's officials and the servants in their robes she was overwhelmed (vs. 5). Everything Solomon did was marked by a spirit of excellence that reflected his reverence for God. His kingdom functioned in uniformity and order, with every detail thoughtfully designed and purposefully executed. Nothing was careless or common and each work displayed the highest quality and intentional craftsmanship. Solomon's life reminds us that excellence honors God and sets a standard that draws others to Him. You grow your reputation by exercising excellence which is the quality of being outstanding. Don't do anything half-heartedly. Do it with excellence, with a high and disciplined standard that glorifies God and pleases Him.

In his later years, Solomon reflected on the brevity of life and urged us not to waste the days God has given us. His words, "Whatever your hand finds to do, do it with your might" (Eccl. 9:10) call us to live with purpose, diligence, and excellence in every assignment. Knowing our time is limited, we honor God by giving our full effort to the work set before us today. Paul said the same thing in Col. 3:23, "And whatever you do, do it heartily, as to the Lord and not to men." He is saying that every task, great or small, is ultimately an act of service to the Lord. When we work with our whole heart, our motivation shifts from pleasing people to honoring God. This mindset brings purpose, excellence, and faithfulness into everything we do. Whatever work you do, do it with enthusiasm and passion. Do it with a spirit of excellence. Having a good attitude toward your work transforms not only your own joy, peace, and fulfillment, but also powerfully influences and uplifts everyone around you.

| 15 |

"GET WISDOM"

The story of Solomon teaches us that a real man is not defined by strength, status, or success but by wisdom. To act like a man, you must get wisdom and understanding. When Solomon was given the opportunity to ask God for anything, he did not ask for wealth, power, or long life. He asked for wisdom and understanding. That choice revealed the heart of a true man. Solomon understood that muscles can fail, riches can vanish, and authority can be abused but wisdom builds a life that lasts. Wisdom gives direction when emotions run high. Understanding brings restraint when pride wants to take control. A man who lacks wisdom may appear strong on the outside, but inwardly he is unstable and easily shaken. True strength is not measured by muscle or bravado, but by discernment, humility, and self-control. Wisdom anchors a man's soul, giving him stability when temptation and trials arise. Scripture tells us, "Get wisdom, get understanding" (Proverbs 4:5). This is not a suggestion. It is a command.

To act like a man is to pursue wisdom intentionally. A wise man listens before he speaks, seeks counsel before he acts, and fears God above all else. He knows that decisions made in haste can destroy years of progress, but decisions made in wisdom establish a legacy. Solomon also teaches us that wisdom begins with humility. He acknowledged his need for God. He knew that leadership without wisdom leads to ruin. The same is true today. A man who refuses correction and ignores instruction is headed for collapse. But a man who seeks God daily for wisdom becomes a pillar - steady, dependable, and respected. In a world that celebrates aggression and ego, God calls men to something higher. Acting like a man means thinking like a man of wisdom. It means choosing understanding over impulse, discipline over pride, and obedience over arrogance. Wisdom protects your family, strengthens your faith, and shapes your future.

If you want to be a real man, follow Solomon's example and ask God for wisdom, pursue understanding, and walk in the fear of the Lord. Strength may win battles in the moment, but wisdom is what guides a life to lasting victory and purpose. Solomon wrote in Prov. 4:7, "Wisdom is the principle thing; therefore, get wisdom. And in all your getting, get understanding." The Message Bible says, "Sell everything and buy wisdom! Never walk away from wisdom - she guards your life; love her - she keeps her eyes on you. Above all and before all, do this: Get wisdom! Write this at the top of your list: get understanding." Wisdom is the proper use of knowledge. It doesn't do any good to know something if you don't apply it properly. Knowledge is information, understanding is comprehension, wisdom is application. A lot of people have head knowledge, but it hasn't become a revelation to them yet. Therefore, they are unable to apply what they have. It's useless to know something if you don't apply it.

More than anything, to grow into a man and to act like a man will require wisdom. You can be very smart but still make a series of stupid, cataclysmic decisions. Men not having godly wisdom is the crisis in our culture. This is one of the biggest problems in the world today. Every day smart people are making stupid decisions because they have no wisdom. The world is filled with educated people but still the earth is in the worst shape it's ever been in. This tells us that going to school and having information doesn't make you wise. The world we live in today is seen in Rom. 1:22, "Claiming to be wise, they instead became utter fools." The Message Bible says, "They pretended to know it all, but were illiterate regarding life." The problem today is the world is filled with smart people doing stupid things. They have knowledge but no wisdom. Knowledge is good but, by itself, it's not enough. Knowledge tells you what you can do, but wisdom shows you how and when to apply it so it produces the right result.

The Bible reminds us that wisdom is a precious jewel, far more valuable and profitable than gold or silver. According to Proverbs 3:13–18, those who find wisdom discover true riches that bring long life, peace, and lasting blessing. Wisdom is a major theme throughout the Bible, emphasized by the fact that the words "wise" and "wisdom" appear over 400 times in scripture. This repetition shows how deeply God values wisdom and calls His people to seek it as a foundation for righteous living and sound decisions. There is a difference between knowledge and wisdom. Knowledge informs the mind by revealing what is true and what to believe. Wisdom transforms the life by guiding how to live, choose, and behave according to that truth. Knowledge gives you facts to learn and information to understand, but wisdom gives you the faith to apply truth to everyday life. Knowledge fills the mind, while wisdom shapes the heart. Knowledge will challenge your mind; wisdom will change your life.

Knowledge gathers facts and understanding, filling the mind with information. Wisdom applies that knowledge to change the heart, shaping how we live, choose, and become. Knowledge can be gained through study, books, and instruction in school. Wisdom, however, is given by the Holy Spirit, guiding us to apply what we know with discernment and truth. When knowledge and the Spirit's wisdom work together, they lead us to live rightly and purposefully. Knowledge equips you with the information and skills needed to succeed in school and achieve good grades. Wisdom teaches you how to apply what you know with understanding, integrity, and purpose so you can live a good and meaningful life. Knowledge is often cherished by the haughty because it elevates the mind and feeds the ego with a sense of superiority. Wisdom, however, is embraced by the humble, for it teaches the heart to listen, learn, and live rightly before God and others. Knowledge is theoretical, wisdom is practical.

The world today needs real men like never before, men of courage, conviction, and character. God made you a man on purpose, with strength to lead, protect, and stand for what is right. It is your responsibility to rise up, reject passivity, and act like the man God created you to be. To act like a man is to pursue wisdom with intention and unwavering resolve. True maturity is revealed when you chase wisdom relentlessly, valuing it above comfort and convenience. A man who gives everything to gain wisdom builds a life that stands firm, honors God, and blesses others. 1 Kings 3 tells us that Solomon loved God and walked with God and worshiped God. Vs. 5 says God appeared to Solomon in a dream and offered to grant him one wish. He said, "Ask for whatever you want me to give you." The first thing Solomon did was thank God for taking care of his father David, for showing him great kindness (vs. 6). Before asking God for what he wants tomorrow, he thanks God for what He did yesterday.

Solomon said next, "I am a little child, I do not know how to go out or come in." Solomon's words reveal a heart of humility, recognizing that wisdom and leadership do not come from age or position but from dependence on God. By calling himself "a little child," he acknowledged his insufficiency and his need for divine guidance in every decision. At about 28 years old, he approaches God with a heart fully surrendered, aware of his dependence and need for divine guidance. His words are marked by a deep, reverent humility that honors God above all else. He says in vs. 8, "And Your servant is in the midst of Your people whom You have chosen, a great people too numerous to be numbered or counted." Not only is he humble but he is also desperate being fully aware that the task before him is far greater than his own strength. He's like a child and it's a huge responsibility to be king over such a vast number of people. He knows he must depend completely on God for wisdom, direction, and understanding.

David has died and the throne of Israel passed to Solomon just as the Lord had promised. With the crown came not only power, but the God-given authority to rule, judge, and lead the nation in wisdom. Solomon now stood responsible to steward that authority faithfully, knowing that true strength flows from obedience to God. At the same time, he is humble enough to confess that the weight of ruling such a great people is beyond his own strength. He recognizes that wisdom, discernment, and justice can only come from God, not from power or position. In that humility, he places his throne under heaven's authority, trusting God to lead where human ability falls short. He then told God the one thing he wanted God to give him. "Give to Your servant an understanding heart to judge Your people, that I may discern between good and evil" (vs. 9). Solomon, fully aware of his dependence on God, humbly asked not for riches or power but for wisdom to lead God's people with discernment and righteousness.

A true qualifier for seeking wisdom is a heart that is thankful, recognizing that every good insight comes from God. It is a humble and desperate posture that admits our own insufficiency and refuses self-reliance. Genuine wisdom is found when we live daily in dependent trust, looking to God alone as our source. What is wisdom? It's having a discerning heart to distinguish between right and wrong, good and evil. James 1:5, "If any of you lacks wisdom, let him ask of God, who gives to all liberally and without reproach, and it will be given to him." If you find yourself lacking wisdom, simply ask God in faith, trusting that He generously gives understanding and guidance to all who seek Him. The Message Bible says, "Ask boldly, believingly, without a second thought." When you approach God with a thankful heart and genuine humility, you position yourself to receive what you truly need. God delights in granting wisdom to those who seek Him not for selfish gain, but to honor Him and serve others well.

Solomon could have asked for wealth, fame, or power, yet he chose something far greater. He understood that wisdom would guide every decision, influence every outcome, and honor God above personal gain. Solomon could have asked for money, fame, and power but he didn't. Instead, he asked for wisdom. Solomon understood that wisdom was the key that unlocked prosperity, authority, and lasting influence. He knew that with God-given wisdom, wealth could be created, power could be exercised rightly, and doors of opportunity would open. Solomon's life shows that wisdom is a divine advantage that shapes success and legacy. God was so pleased with his answer that He gave Solomon not only wisdom but wealth, power, and influence. He gave him everything. The truth is, once you get wisdom, God can then provide the rest. Godly and wise men build strong marriages, raise faithful and honorable children, and leave behind a lasting legacy that honors God and blesses generations.

Wisdom helps you grow up and mature, shaping your character so you are no longer driven by impulse but by understanding. As wisdom increases, it prepares you to carry greater responsibilities with humility, discipline, and discernment. In this way, wisdom enables you to handle every assignment in a godly manner that honors God and blesses others. Learn the lessons of wisdom the Bible teaches you, for God's Word equips you to walk with discernment, humility, and strength. Move forward in faith, taking responsibility for your choices and living out obedience with courage and integrity. Finish your race well by remaining steadfast, disciplined, and focused on honoring God to the very end. Stand firm in the faith, holding tightly to God's truth even when circumstances try to shake you. As you remain grounded in what you believe, His wisdom shapes your thoughts, decisions, and reactions. That steady faith equips you to handle the everyday issues of life with clarity, strength, and peace.

God is offering us wisdom so how do we get it? Godly wisdom is a precious gift given by the Holy Spirit, not something earned by human effort or intellect. It is poured into the hearts of the children of God, guiding them to think, choose, and live according to God's truth. This wisdom brings clarity in confusion, peace in trials, and discernment in a noisy world. Those who walk in fellowship with God have access to a wisdom that leads to life, righteousness, and lasting fruit. Paul prayed "that the God of our Lord Jesus Christ, the Father of glory, may give to you the spirit of wisdom and revelation in the knowledge of Him" (Eph. 1:17). The Holy Spirit brings wisdom. You don't have to be smart to be wise. You just need the Holy Spirit. Is.

30:21 says, "Whether you turn to the right or to the left, your eyes will hear a voice behind you, saying, 'This is the way; walk in it.'" Sometimes, when you need wisdom to make a certain decision, God will speak to you in a still, small voice (1 Kings 19:12).

You will know deep inside your inner man when it is God speaking to you because His voice brings peace, clarity, and alignment with His Word. Jesus said, "My sheep hear My voice" (John 10:27), reminding us that a living relationship with Him includes spiritual recognition, not confusion. As you walk closely with Christ, His guidance becomes familiar, steady, and unmistakable. Most times, His voice is connected to His Word. He'll remind you of something you've read in the Bible that pertains to the situation you are in. Wisdom also comes from prayer and worship. Bring your burdens to God and ask Him for wisdom. It comes from your conscience, your intuition. You'll just know if something is a good or bad idea. Some things aren't sinful, they're just stupid. Your experience in life also brings wisdom. If you do something and it didn't work out, don't do it a second time. Learn from your experience by allowing every failure to become a teacher that shapes your wisdom and strengthens your character.

Wisdom is not gained in isolation, for God often speaks through the counsel of other wise men who have walked the path before us. When we listen humbly to godly advice, our understanding is sharpened and our blind spots are revealed. In the multitude of wise counselors, discernment grows stronger and decisions are established with confidence. Prov. 13:20 says,

"Whoever walks with the wise becomes wise, but the companion of fools will suffer harm." Find men whose wisdom exceeds your own and choose to walk beside them with humility and intention. Listen closely as they speak, watch how they live, and allow their experience to shape your thinking and character. Wisdom is not only learned - it is imparted through fellowship, example, and a teachable spirit. An ancient proverb says, "Show me your friends and I'll show you your future." Prov. 15:22 says, "Without counsel, plans go awry, but in the multitude of counselors they are established."

The ministry of the Holy Spirit in a man is to fill him with divine wisdom and holy power, shaping his thoughts, actions, and desires. Through the Spirit's guidance and strength, a man is transformed from within, learning to walk as Jesus walked. This work of the Holy Spirit produces Christlike character, bold faith, and a life that reflects the heart of Jesus to the world. Luke 2:40 says, "Jesus grew and became strong in spirit, filled with wisdom." This reminds us that spiritual growth is intentional. Jesus matured as His spirit grew strong and wisdom continually shaped His life. It shows us that true strength is developed through obedience, time with God, and a heart willing to grow. At age 12, Jesus was found in the temple, sitting in the midst of the teachers, listening to them and asking them questions. What's He doing? He's finding men who were older than Him and He's building relationships with them. Luke 2:47 says, "And all who heard Him were astonished at His understanding and answers.

Why were they astonished? Because even at twelve years old, His words carried depth, insight, and divine understanding beyond His years. He spoke with wisdom that could not be explained by education alone, revealing a heart fully aligned with God. In Him, they witnessed not just a child, but the unmistakable presence of heavenly wisdom at work. Luke 2:52, "And Jesus increased in wisdom and stature, and in favor with God and man." Even Jesus embraced a life of continual growth, developing in wisdom, strength, and maturity. His example shows us that spiritual life is not stagnant but meant to progress in alignment with God's will. As Jesus grew in favor with God, He modeled obedience, humility, and a deepening relationship with the Father. As He grew in favor with man, He demonstrated character, compassion, and integrity that drew others toward God. To truly act like a man, you must do the same thing - stand firm and live out your convictions with courage and integrity.

God the Father sent Jesus to the earth to reveal His heart and to show humanity what true wisdom looks like in daily life. Through Jesus' words, actions, humility, and obedience, we see how a wise man walks in love, truth, and submission to God. By following Christ's example, we learn not only what to believe, but how to live wisely before God and others. Jesus was fully God and fully man and He lived by the power of the Holy Spirit. He was filled with the Holy Spirit, was always learning, was always growing in wisdom. People ask, "How can we be like Jesus?" By the power of the Holy Spirit. The Holy Spirit is at work in you right now, shaping your heart, renewing your mind, and teaching you how to live with the wisdom and maturity of Jesus. No matter what stage of life you are in, He patiently guides you to grow, discern rightly, and reflect Christ more fully each day. What does wisdom look like? It looks like the Holy Spirit shaping your heart, character, and decisions to reflect the likeness of Jesus.

| 16 |

"BE STRONG"

The closing words of a letter often reveal what matters most. As the Apostle Paul closes his first letter to the church at Corinth, he does not end with soft words or gentle suggestions. Instead, he issues a clear, commanding call meant to echo through every generation of believers. Paul writes to a church surrounded by confusion, compromise, division, and moral weakness. Corinth was a city overflowing with wealth, pleasure, and intellectual pride, yet bankrupt in spiritual discipline. In this environment, Paul does not tell the church to blend in, relax, or retreat. He tells them to stand, to watch, and above all to be strong. This is not a message reserved for pastors, leaders, or a select few. It is a mandate for every believer, and it carries a particular weight for men who are often called to lead, protect, and endure in both family and faith. To "be strong" is not a suggestion. It is a command. God calls all men who claim to be His to stand firm, act courageously, and live out the strength He has already supplied.

When Paul says, "be strong," he is not speaking of physical dominance, emotional hardness, or human self-confidence. Biblical strength is not loud, aggressive, or arrogant. True strength is anchored in God, not ego. Biblical strength is spiritual resilience - the ability to remain faithful under pressure, obedient in adversity, and courageous when compromise would be easier. It is strength that endures when feelings fail, stands when culture shifts, obeys when obedience costs, remains faithful when no one is watching. The life of a man of God is not passive or comfortable - it is an active participation in a spiritual battle fought daily against the world, the flesh, and the devil. He stands alert and disciplined, clothed in faith and truth, knowing that victory comes not by strength alone but by obedience to God. Know with certainty that the opposition is real and the warfare intense. This is why after telling us to "act like men" in 1 Cor. 16:13, Paul next commands us to "be strong."

Real men of God are called to be spiritually strong, standing firm in faith regardless of pressure or opposition. This strength is cultivated through watchfulness, through remaining alert, prayerful, and grounded in God's truth. It is sustained by stability, refusing to be moved by fear, compromise, or cultural drift. True manliness is revealed when a man courageously lives out his faith with conviction, discipline, and unwavering obedience to God. Paul is calling men to more than outward masculinity. He is urging them to be mighty in the inner man. He understood that true strength is forged in the heart, where faith, courage, and obedience are formed. God designed men to be strong, not merely in body, but in spirit, resolve, and conviction. When a man is strengthened inwardly by God, he is equipped to stand firm, lead boldly, and endure faithfully. God placed a warrior spirit deep within every man's heart to be summoned with strength, courage, and restraint when the moment truly demands it.

Eph. 3:16 (NLT) says, "I pray that from His glorious, unlimited resources He will empower you with inner strength through His Spirit." God's strength for your life does not come from your own effort, but from His glorious and unlimited resources. When you rely on the Holy Spirit, He empowers you from the inside out, giving you courage, endurance, and stability no matter the circumstance. This inner strength enables you to stand firm, live boldly, and walk faithfully in God's purpose. The Message Bible says this is "not a brute strength but a glorious inner strength" that comes from God. Only when we abide in the Lord and live in union with Him do we possess the true power to overcome the enemy. Apart from Christ we are vulnerable, but in Him we stand strengthened, victorious, and fully equipped to prevail. Separated from Christ, we are utterly powerless but in Him we have access to the immeasurable power of His might, enabling us to overcome every obstacle, and accomplish all He has called us to do.

Paul begins his command with the word "watch. Strength is impossible without awareness, because you cannot confront what you refuse to recognize. A man who is not watchful leaves his life unguarded, making him vulnerable to temptation, distraction, laziness, and deception. Strength of character is sustained by alertness, for what is not guarded will eventually be overtaken. Spiritual strength requires alertness - an intentional watchfulness over your life so nothing slips in unnoticed. It means guarding your heart from compromise, your mind from deception, your doctrine from distortion, and your devotion from growing cold. A strong believer stays awake in spirit, standing firm in truth and faithful in love. The enemy does not announce his arrival. He creeps in, he distracts, and he deceives. To be strong, a man must first be awake because awareness creates the ground where real strength is forged. Until a man sees clearly where he stands, he will never have the power to move forward with purpose.

Paul continues his exhortation by saying, "Stand firm in the faith." Strength is not proven by constant movement or endless change, but by the ability to stand firm when the winds blow. True strength comes from having your feet planted on solid ground, rooted in truth, character, and faith. When you are grounded, you remain unshaken, steady, and secure. The world is constantly redefining truth, reshaping morality, and challenging biblical convictions. A strong man does not drift with cultural currents; he anchors himself in eternal truth. While opinions shift and values fade, his life remains steady because it is rooted in what never changes. To stand fast means refusing to bend scripture to fit society, holding conviction even when it isolates you, remaining faithful even when truth is unpopular. Standing firm takes strength because pressure never stops pushing even when no one else sees it. True strength is proven not by escaping the pressure, but by remaining firm and unmoved while it presses in.

The phrase "act like men" is an old expression that calls for courage, maturity, and responsibility in how one lives and responds to life's challenges. It speaks to standing firm in character, doing what is right even when it is difficult, and taking ownership of one's actions. At its heart, it is a call to strength of spirit, integrity of heart, and faithfulness in purpose. Paul is not appealing to masculinity as culture defines it, but to spiritual maturity. This is a call to grow up in faith leaving behind passivity, excuses, and spiritual immaturity, and stepping into intentional, disciplined obedience. God is calling all men to stand strong, take responsibility for their walk, and live with courage, conviction, and maturity in Christ. Men who never grow up and mature will never be strong, because strength is developed through growth, testing, and obedience. Immature men shrink back at pressure, but men who are strong learn to trust God beyond their fickle feelings and their circumstances that go against the will of God.

True strength is revealed over time, not in the excitement of beginnings but in the discipline of endurance. Anyone can start strong when motivation is high and the path is clear. Few finish strong because finishing demands character, perseverance, and faith when the journey becomes difficult. True strength is revealed not at the start, but in the resolve to press on when quitting would be easier. Strength that lasts is forged by consistency, obedience, and the resolve to stand firm until the end. Paul's life itself testifies to this truth. He endured persecution, imprisonment, rejection, hardship, and suffering yet he remained faithful. His strength was not rooted in comfort, but in his calling. Shortly before his death he wrote, "I have fought a good fight, I have finished my course, I have kept the faith" (2 Tim. 4:7). Strength is proven by how faithfully you live when life becomes difficult. Real men stand firm in quiet obedience, persevering with unwavering trust in God when no one is watching and the road is hard.

Where does strength come from? Strength comes from God. Ps. 37:39 says, "Salvation is from the Lord, He is their strength in times of trouble." God sees every weary soul and never despises our weakness; instead, He meets us there with His power. When our strength is gone and our resolve feels empty, Is. 40:29 says, "He gives power to the weak, and to those who have no might He increases strength." This verse reminds us that God Himself supplies what we lack. In surrender, the weak become strong not by their own might, but by the unfailing strength of the Lord. No man produces this strength on his own. Paul understood that human strength fails quickly, but God's strength never does. In 2 Cor. 12:9 he quoted what God said to him during a time of struggle, "My grace is sufficient for thee; for My strength is made [/perfect in weakness. The strength Paul commands is received, not manufactured. When a man admits his weakness, God supplies His strength.

God calls every man to walk in a strength that flows from complete dependence on Him. True strength is found when a man humbles himself before God and allows the Lord to be his source. When God supplies the strength, it endures pressure, overcomes weakness, and stands firm in adversity. A man who draws his strength from God does not merely survive life's battles - he walks in victory through them. In Joshua 1:9, the Lord commands us to be strong and courageous, reminding us that divine strength is not optional but expected. When a man leans on God's presence, he can stand firm, fearless, and unwavering in every challenge. Ps. 31:24 says, "Be of good courage and he shall strengthen your heart." Be of good courage because God sees your faith even when the way feels uncertain. As you trust Him, He will strengthen your heart with divine strength that goes beyond your own. Stand firm in hope, knowing that the Lord renews those who boldly place their confidence in Him.

God is looking for men to give strength to, men who will let Him make them strong. 2 Chron. 16:9, "For the eyes of the Lord run to and fro throughout the whole earth, to show Himself strong on behalf of those whose heart is loyal to Him." God is looking for men humble enough to admit their need for Him. He is not searching for the self-sufficient; He is searching for the surrendered. Strength in God's kingdom is not produced by pride, talent, or sheer willpower, but by a heart that is fully yielded to Him. Many men spend their lives trying to prove how strong they are, yet God is looking for men willing to confess how weak they feel without Him. When a man stops striving in his own ability and begins trusting in God's power, something supernatural happens. God steps in where human strength ends. He does not shame weakness; He fills it. He does not despise brokenness; He rebuilds it. A man who allows God to make him strong becomes anchored, steady, and unshakeable.

God's strength is not merely physical or emotional; it is spiritual, moral, and enduring. It empowers a man to stand firm when temptation pulls hard, to remain faithful when culture drifts, and to lead with courage when fear whispers retreat. This strength teaches a man how to love sacrificially, forgive deeply, endure patiently, and obey fully. It produces integrity in private, boldness in public, and consistency in daily life. The men God strengthens are not perfect, but they are available. They are men who pray instead of pretending, who kneel before they stand, and who depend on God daily rather than calling on Him only in crisis. They understand that true manhood is not about domination, ego, or control, but about submission to God's will and alignment with His purpose. When a man gives God access to his heart, God gives that man access to His strength. In a world desperate for real leaders, God is still raising up men who will let Him shape their character and supply their power.

These are the men who become pillars in their homes, examples in their communities, and warriors in the spiritual realm. Their strength is not loud, but it is lasting. It is not flashy, but it is faithful. And it does not come from themselves - it comes from the Lord who delights in making willing men strong. When a man truly gives God access to his heart, something profound begins to happen beneath the surface of his life. This is not a casual invitation or a surface-level acknowledgment of God's existence; it is a surrender of the inner man - the thoughts, motives, fears, wounds, and ambitions that shape who he really is. Scripture reminds us that "man looks at the outward appearance, but the Lord looks at the heart" (1 Sam. 16:7). When a man opens his heart to God, he invites the One who sees fully and knows completely to take rightful authority over his life. True strength is not found in our own ability, but in humbly trusting God's wisdom to guide and direct every step we take.

The heart is the control center of a man's strength or weakness. Guarded hearts breed self-reliance, pride, and hidden insecurity, but surrendered hearts cultivate humility, trust, and obedience. When a man insists on protecting his heart from God, he is left to rely on his own limited strength. Human strength is temporary, easily exhausted, and often fueled by ego or fear. But when a man lays down his defenses and says, "Lord, search me, lead me, and rule me," he exchanges fragile self-effort for divine empowerment. God never forces His strength upon a man; He responds to invitation and surrender. Throughout scripture, God's power flows through yielded men who understood their limitations and trusted God's sufficiency. David was not strong because of his size or skill, but because his heart belonged to God. When his heart was aligned, God's strength rested upon him. The same is true today: access to God's strength follows access to the man's heart.

When God has access to a man's heart, He begins to strengthen him from the inside out. This strength is not merely physical or emotional; it is spiritual fortitude. It is the strength to stand when pressure mounts, to remain faithful when compromise looks easier, to love when bitterness would be justified, and to persevere when circumstances threaten to break him. God's strength steadies a man's mind, anchors his emotions, and fortifies his spirit. This divine strength also brings clarity and courage. A man with God's strength does not live in constant reaction to fear or opinion. He becomes secure in identity and firm in conviction. He no longer needs to prove himself to others because he knows whom he belongs to. God's strength produces quiet confidence - a calm resolve that does not boast loudly but stands unshaken. This is the strength that enables a man to lead his family with wisdom, serve others with compassion, and walk in integrity when no one is watching.

God's strength is not given for comfort alone; it is given for purpose. A man strengthened by God is empowered to fulfill his calling. He is equipped to fight spiritual battles, to resist temptation, and to walk in obedience even when the path is costly. This strength does not make life easy, but it makes a man unmovable. When storms come God's strength keeps him standing, rooted, and faithful. Ultimately, when a man gives God access to his heart, he discovers that God's strength is not a resource to be borrowed occasionally, but a life to be lived daily. It becomes a constant supply, renewed moment by moment through prayer, obedience, and trust. The man who walks in this truth no longer says, "I can't," but instead declares, "I can do all things through Christ who strengthens me." His life becomes living proof that surrender is not weakness - it is the gateway to divine strength. When a man yields his will to God, he rises empowered by a strength far greater than his own.

This command to "be strong" is just as urgent today as it was in Corinth. This is not a call to loud bravado or self-reliance, but to a settled, watchful strength rooted in Christ. To "be strong" is to stand firm when compromise beckons, to remain alert when spiritual dullness threatens, and to act with courage when obedience carries a cost. This strength is forged in faith - daily choosing truth over comfort, conviction over convenience, and God's will over personal gain. It is the kind of strength that does not retreat under pressure but rises with clarity and resolve, anchored in the unchanging power of God. The church does not need weaker men. Families do not need passive leaders. The world does not need silent believers. God is calling all men to watch carefully, stand firmly, live courageously, love deeply, and be strong in the Lord. Strength is not optional - it is the God-given resolve that empowers faithfulness, anchors true leadership, and secures a lasting legacy.

Paul's command is not a suggestion - it is a call to arms. Spiritual strength is not passive, emotional, or occasional; it is deliberate, disciplined, and anchored in truth. Always remember that biblical strength is sustained by love and expressed through faithful action. A man who stands watchful, courageous, and steadfast becomes a living testimony of God's power at work within him. When weakness appears, it becomes an invitation to rely more fully on the Lord, for true strength is perfected through dependence on Him. Stand firm. Stay alert. Act like men of God. And in every season, draw your strength from the One who never falters. As the world draws to a close, the challenge remains: will you answer Paul's command? Spiritual strength is not inherited - it is cultivated. It grows through prayer, obedience, endurance, and daily submission to God. Stand firm. Stay alert. Act like a man of God. Be strong not in yourself, but in the power of the Lord who equips, sustains, and calls you to live boldly for His glory.

| 17 |

"A FORCE OF NATURE"

In the Bible, the word "strength" is mentioned 360 times. Most often it is linked to God's power. In other words, the unlimited power of Christ is the source of strength for those who belong to Him. When our ability ends, His power remains unshaken, supplying what we could never produce on our own. Those who abide in Christ do not live by human strength, but by divine power that never fails. Hab. 3:19 says, "The Lord God is my strength; He will make my feet like deer's feet, and He will make me walk on my high hills." By faith, you can live with unshakable assurance that God's strength is real, present, and active in your life. What He provides is not only available in every moment but fully sufficient for every challenge you face. You don't have to be strong in order to have His strength. It's when you're weak that God's strength shows up. God told Paul in 2 Cor. 12:9 (MSG), "My grace is enough; it's all you need. My strength comes into its own in your weakness."

God calls you to be strong in His strength, not to become strong so that you can earn it. His power is not a reward for self-effort, but a gift freely given to those who trust and depend on Him. When you stop striving in your own ability and rest in His, His strength works fully in you. Paul did not respond to God's word by striving harder, but by surrendering more fully to His grace. He embraced the truth that his weakness created space for Christ's power to rest upon him. In accepting God's answer, Paul declared, "For when I am weak, then I am strong" (vs. 10) because strength is found in dependence, not self-reliance. Those who rely on God's strength discover that He is a never-ending source of power, renewal, and endurance. In every season, His strength sustains, energizes, and carries them beyond what they could ever accomplish on their own. He'll give you strength to minister to others (1 Tim. 1:12), strength to face persecution (2 Tim. 1:8), and strength to overcome death (1 Cor. 15:57).

Eph. 6:10 says, "Finally, my brethren, be strong in the Lord and in the power of His might." The Greek word for "be strong" is "endunamoo." It's made up of the Greek words "en" and "dunamis." The word "en" means 'in' and "dunamis" is the Greek word for 'power.' The word "dunamis" was used to describe the force of nature, like a hurricane or an earthquake. It was also used to describe the full might of an invading army. Paul is saying that the power of the Holy Spirit is not a passive influence but a divine force of nature, active and unstoppable. It works with transforming power in the lives of men, shaping them from the inside out according to God's will. He comes like a tornado, like a mighty rushing wind (Acts

2:2), unstoppable, life-changing, and powerful enough to shake everything that stands in the way of God's purpose. In other words, He comes to shake things up. The Greek word "endunamoo" means 'to put power in a human vessel,' much like pouring water into a vase.

The term "be strong" is not a suggestion of self-effort, but a divine transfer of strength. It depicts the power of an entire army being deposited into one person. It speaks of God infusing courage, endurance, authority, and resolve far beyond human capacity. To "be strong" is to stand carrying heaven's force within you, ready to advance, endure, and overcome. It speaks of an inner strengthening that goes beyond human resolve - a supernatural enablement released by God Himself. This power does not merely sustain; it ignites, producing an explosive, superhuman strength charged with divine energy. It empowers a person to stand, endure, and advance far beyond natural limits. Being strong is not optional for men of God. It is not a personality trait reserved for the bold or the naturally confident. It is not a suggestion, and it is certainly not a cultural stereotype. Scripture does not say some men should be strong. It commands that all men are to be strong in the Lord and in the power of His might.

This command immediately shifts our understanding of strength. God is not calling men to manufacture power from within themselves. He is calling men to draw strength from Him. Biblical strength is not about physical dominance, emotional suppression, or stubborn self-reliance. It is about dependence upon divine power. The world tells men to be strong by being self-sufficient. God tells men to be strong by being God-sufficient. The paradox of spiritual strength is that it begins where pride ends. Many men struggle with this truth because surrender feels like weakness. But in the kingdom of God, surrender is the doorway to power. When a man finally admits, "I cannot do this on my own," he positions himself to receive strength beyond himself. God's strength is not added to our strength; it replaces it so that what is accomplished is not by our power, but by His. Only when a man stops trusting his own ability does he begin to experience the power of God operating through him.

Men are not strong because they attend church. They are strong because they walk with God. Spiritual strength is not built in moments of public worship alone but in the quiet, unseen disciplines of daily devotion. A man who is strong in the Lord is a man who prays when no one is watching and reads the Word not for information, but for transformation. He obeys God even when obedience costs him comfort, repents quickly and humbly, and refuses to compromise truth for acceptance. The strength of a man's public life is always determined by the depth of his private life with God. What is built in secret shapes what is sustained in the spotlight. When a man is rooted in prayer, obedience, and quiet faithfulness, his leadership carries integrity and endurance. Public influence may impress people, but private devotion is what empowers a life that truly honors God. When a man walks faithfully with God in secret, his public life carries authentic strength, integrity, and lasting spiritual impact.

God calls men to be strong because life is a battleground, and only those anchored in His truth and courage can finish faithful. Spiritual strength is required because spiritual opposition is real. Men face attacks against their faith, integrity, marriages, purity, leadership, and calling. The enemy does not fear a man who is talented, successful, or charismatic. He fears a man who is submitted, armored, and dependent on God. Notice that Paul did not command you to be strong in yourself but in the power of His might. This distinction is critical. Human strength is limited. It grows tired. It fails under pressure. It breaks under temptation. But God's might never diminishes. The same power that spoke creation into existence, parted the Red Sea, raised Christ from the dead, and defeated sin and death now resides within the man of God through the Holy Spirit. Men do not lack strength because God has withheld it. They lack strength because they have tried to fight spiritual battles with their own strength.

Men are not strengthened by God for themselves alone. They are strengthened so they can lead, protect, and serve others. Families rise or fall on the strength of the men who lead them spiritually. Churches are strengthened when men stand in faith. Communities are transformed when godly men refuse to retreat. A strong man lifts others. He encourages the weak. He mentors the young. He stands in the gap for those who cannot stand for themselves. He does not use strength to dominate but to serve. The Bible is filled with men who were not strong in themselves, but strong in God, men like David, Gideon, Moses, Paul. Their strength came not from stature, background, or natural ability, but from their reliance on the Lord. God is still calling men today to rise in spiritual strength. Not strength that boasts, but strength that bows. Not strength that intimidates, but strength that endures. Not strength that seeks recognition, but strength that brings God glory, strength is found in Him alone.

God's divine power working within you is what it truly means to be strong in the Lord and in the power of His might. This strength is not human effort or self-reliance, but the living presence of God empowering your faith, courage, and obedience. When you walk in His power, you stand firm, overcome adversity, and fulfill His purpose with confidence and authority. It's the "dunamis" power that produces phenomenal, extra-ordinary, unparalleled results. The Lord's power dwelling inside of us makes us able and fully capable for every calling He gives. His strength supplies everything we need for any task before us. When we rely on His power, we move forward not in our own ability, but in His unstoppable strength. Our responsibility is to take on the world's challenges with strength, knowing that our strength comes from God and not ourselves. God wants men to protect their wives and children and all the innocent people around them who can't protect themselves.

1 Tim. 1:12 says, "I thank Christ Jesus our Lord, who has strengthened me, because He considered me fruitful, putting me into service." God is faithful and gracious. He sees beyond our past and our weaknesses and calls us to be fruitful by His power, not our performance. Being placed into His service is both a gift and a responsibility. All men are to live strength-

ened by God and faithful to the calling He has entrusted to them. 2 Sam. 10:12, "Be strong and let us show ourselves courageous for the sake of our people and for the cities of our God." Strong men are on the earth to get the job done whether the work is dirty, dangerous, or difficult. They step forward when others hesitate, shouldering responsibility with courage, endurance, and unwavering resolve. In doing so, they become the steady pillars others lean on. Clergyman Phillips Brooks said in the 19th century, "Do not pray for easy lives! Pray to be stronger men. Do not pray for tasks equal to your power, pray for power equal to your tasks."

God placed His mighty "dunamis" power within your inner man so you would not live weak, fearful, or defeated. This divine power strengthens your spirit, renews your mind, and equips you to stand firm in faith no matter the opposition. What God placed inside you is more than enough to overcome, endure, and fulfill His purpose for your life. You are the container God has chosen, fearfully and wonderfully made to carry His presence and purpose. Within you dwells divine power - not by your own strength, but by the Spirit of the living God working through you. When you walk in faith and obedience, what He placed inside you is released to change lives, shape destiny, and bring Him glory. Receiving this power is not an option. You are being commanded to be strong in the Lord. To act like a man, you must receive inside of you a supernatural deposit of power. When this happens, weak men become mighty warriors of God. They become strong and powerful. They become superhuman beings.

When you receive this power inside of you, a supernatural transformation takes place that reaches far beyond the surface of your life. What once limited you no longer defines you, because divine strength begins to renew your mind, reshape your character, and realign your purpose. You are not merely improved - you are inwardly changed, empowered to live, lead, and love in a way that reflects God's power at work within you. Normal men become supernatural men when they surrender their ordinary strength to an extraordinary God. What once relied on flesh and willpower alone is transformed by faith, obedience, and divine empowerment. Through God, men rise above natural limits and accomplish superhuman things that leave a lasting legacy. We're not here to play, we're here to work hard for the kingdom of God. We're here to act like a man and do what needs to be done. Greatness comes not by having a smooth path to walk on, it comes by making a new path with our own hands.

Where does this power come from? Phil. 2:13 (NLT) says, "For God is working in you, giving you the desire and the power to do what pleases Him." The strength to act like a man is not produced by willpower alone, but by the power of God working in the inner man. When God strengthens the heart, courage rises, conviction becomes firm, and obedience follows without compromise. True manhood flows from an inward transformation that empowers outward action. This power works deep within you, shaping your character and igniting a holy passion that transforms who you are from the inside out. It drives you to rise into the strength, discipline, and purpose of the real man God created you to be. This power is not obtained by merely reading books or attending church services. It is not a formula or a ritual to be mastered. True power is found exclusively in the person of Jesus Christ, and it is released through a living, surrendered relationship with Him.

Paul emphasizes seven times in Ephesians 1 that believers are in the Lord, revealing a divine union where Christ lives in you and you live in Him. This truth declares that your identity, authority, and inheritance flow from being inseparably joined to Jesus Christ. You are in the Lord. You're locked up in the person of Jesus. He's a part of you, you're a part of Him. In Him resides all this divine power and strength. If Jesus is in your heart, then this supernatural power is there also. You are immersed in this power twenty-four hours a day, seven days a week, fifty-two weeks a year. You are in Christ, and in Him dwells all authority, strength, and resurrection power. By faith, that power is already present and available - waiting to be received, trusted, and walked out in your life. All you have to do is embrace it and receive it by faith. Nothing more, nothing less. Do that and you will be filled and empowered with God's own divine power working within you, strengthening you to live boldly, faithfully, and victoriously.

Receiving this power is not difficult; God has already made it available to you. All you have to do is receive it by faith, trusting His promise rather than your own strength. It is yours for the taking so step forward and walk in what He has freely given. Remember, you are commanded to do this. You are commanded to be strong not in human ability alone, but through the transforming power of God working within you.

As you yield to that power, you are changed from the ordinary into a supernaturally empowered person, equipped to overcome, endure, and fulfill your calling. Not only that, but you are also commanded to be strong in the power of His might, not in your own weakness or effort. His strength is divine, unlimited, and available to you right now - meant to clothe you with courage, endurance, and authority to stand and overcome. In Greek, the word "power" means 'strength, power, victory over something, taking something by force.' It is demonstrated power, a power that is eruptive and tangible.

This power always comes with an outward manifestation. It's a power you can see, feel, and experience. It is never hidden for it always reveals itself through visible change and tangible impact. You can see it and feel it. You can see it in transformed lives, feel it in renewed strength, and experience it in bold, decisive action. When this power is present, it leaves undeniable evidence that something real has taken place. Signs and wonders follow those who receive the power that comes with being filled with the Holy Spirit, because God's power is never meant to remain hidden or inactive. When the Spirit fills a believer, heaven's authority is released on earth, producing visible evidence that points people to Christ. This power confirms the Word, strengthens faith, and reveals that God is alive, present, and still working today. Jesus said in Acts 1:8, "You shall receive power when the Holy Spirit has come upon you." This is the same power that raised Jesus from the dead, and it resides in you!

The Bible does not merely encourage strength - it commands you to be strong in the power of His might, not your own. This strength is drawn from daily dependence on God, forged through faith, obedience, and surrender to His authority. When you stand in His might, you are equipped to endure trials, lead with courage, and fulfill your God-given calling. The Greek word for "might" is "ischuos" and it refers to 'a strong man, such as a mighty man with great muscular capabilities.' It's a picture of power and strength - great might unleashed with purpose, great force restrained by wisdom, and great ability directed with intention. True strength is not merely what you can do, but what you are capable of carrying, commanding, and sustaining without compromise. This word is used to picture God as One who is able, mighty, and muscular. It describes one who possesses all the might, strength, and ability necessary to overcome any foe and to accomplish every act required.

Indeed, God is mighty and powerful. He created the entire universe, parted the Red Sea, made the earth stand still. God raised Jesus from the dead by His mighty power, proving that death itself could not stand against His authority. That same resurrection power is at work in you, and in Him you have been made a mighty man of valor, called to live boldly, courageously, and victoriously. When you are born again, you are connected to the mighty power of God, a living force that now flows through your life. This divine power strengthens, guides, and enables you to walk in victory and purpose beyond your own ability. Be strong in the powerful, outwardly ability that works within you, not by human effort alone but by the mighty force

God Himself supplies. His great, muscular strength energizes your spirit, enabling you to stand firm, act boldly, and accomplish what would otherwise be impossible. Act like a man and be strong in the Lord wherever you go and whatever you do.

| 18 |

"WALK IN LOVE"

The world today is growing more angry, hostile, and divided as fear, pride, and selfishness drive people further apart. Unfortunately, this same type of behavior is slowly making its way into our homes and churches, eroding peace, trust, and unity from within. What is tolerated in small doses soon becomes normalized, and if left unchecked, it will weaken families, divide congregations, and dull our witness to a watching world. That's why we're here. The real men of God are commanded to stop this from happening. They're called to stand in the gap when chaos, compromise, and corruption try to take ground. We are commanded not to retreat in silence, but to confront darkness with truth, courage, and unwavering conviction. This is our assignment: to protect what is sacred, restore what is broken, and lead with strength anchored in righteousness. How do we do this? 1 Cor. 16:14 tells us, "Let all that you do be done in love." We're to be watchful in love, stand firm in love, act like men in love, be strong in love.

Love brings balance to everything we do as men, shaping our strength with purpose and our actions with wisdom. It keeps our maturity from becoming harsh, tempering power with humility, patience, and compassion. When love leads, our strength remains firm yet gentle, and our leadership becomes both considerate and life-giving. John MacArthur says love "keeps our firmness from becoming hardness and our strength from becoming domineering." Everything we do must be carried out in an atmosphere of unconditional, God-like, God-enabled love that reflects His heart and character. When love leads our actions, it transforms our words, strengthens our purpose, and allows God's power to work through us with grace and truth. Not only is love to reign in our hearts, but it must also shine forth in what we say and the things we do. A Christian man should never be known as an angry or selfish person. The one thing that should characterize our lives is that we walk in love.

Love is to be the distinguishing mark of all men who call Jesus their Lord and Savior, revealing His presence in their hearts through their actions. It is not merely spoken, but lived out in humility, sacrifice, forgiveness, and compassion toward others. When love leads our words and deeds, the world recognizes Christ in us and is drawn to the truth we profess. Jesus said, "This is My commandment, that you love one another as I have loved you" (John 13:34). This command calls us to a higher standard of love - one modeled by sacrifice, humility, and grace. When we love others as He has loved us, we reflect Christ to the world and fulfill the true mark of His disciples. Indeed, love is your highest calling - the clearest expression of God's nature working through your life. When you choose to love, you make the greatest contribution possible, leaving a lasting impact that transforms hearts and builds eternal value. As the world becomes harsher and more divided, our calling to walk in love will make us more distinct.

Love is the answer to every problem in the world not because it ignores truth, justice, or responsibility, but because it addresses the root of every human brokenness. Every war, every division, every act of cruelty, pride, greed, hatred, and injustice can be traced back to a lack of love or a distortion of it. Where love is absent, fear takes over. Where love grows cold, selfishness rules. But where genuine, selfless love is present, healing begins. Love has the power to soften hardened hearts, restore broken relationships, calm angry spirits, and bring light into the darkest places of the human soul. Love is more than emotion or sentiment; it is a daily choice to value others above self, to extend grace when it is undeserved, and to pursue peace even when it is costly. Love listens before it speaks, forgives before it condemns, and serves without demanding recognition. It does not excuse wrongdoing, but it seeks redemption instead of revenge. Love stands firm in truth while remaining gentle in spirit.

Pray continually that your love will deepen, mature, and expand for in a world desperate for answers, love remains the greatest one of all. When you pray that your love for others will increase each day, you are asking God to reshape your heart. You are asking Him to remove bitterness, impatience, pride, and judgment, and to replace them with compassion, humility, and mercy. You are praying to see people not as obstacles or enemies, but as souls created in the image of God, each carrying unseen wounds and silent battles. An increasing love means learning to respond instead of reacting, to bless instead of curse, and to give instead of withholding. A world transformed by love begins with individuals who choose it daily - in homes, churches, workplaces, communities, and even toward strangers. Love that is expressed in small, faithful actions has a ripple effect that reaches far beyond what we can see. A compassionate act can change the course of a life. As love grows in us, peace grows around us.

Commit yourself fully to walking in love every single day. Love is not something you stumble into by accident; it is a choice you make before the day begins and a posture you maintain as the day unfolds. Decide in advance that love will govern your words, your reactions, your tone, and your treatment of others. When pressures rise and patience is tested, say out loud, "I will walk in love." Love is the highest road, the strongest response, and the clearest evidence of spiritual maturity. Give yourself to love without holding back. Do not offer it sparingly or only when it feels convenient. Pour yourself into love the way a servant pours water into a basin freely, humbly, and intentionally. Love is not weakness; it is disciplined strength under control. It requires courage to love when misunderstood, endurance to love when unappreciated, and humility to love when wronged. Yet this kind of love transforms both the giver and the receiver. Seek love as a daily pursuit. Wake up asking, "Who can I show love to today."

Look for opportunities to encourage, to forgive, to listen, to serve, and to show kindness. Love is often found in small, unseen moments, in a gentle word, a patient pause, a quiet act of generosity. Those who seek love will always find it, because love is never far from those who are willing to walk in it. Pursue love with intention and persistence. Chase it even when your emotions resist. Follow after it when offense tries to pull you in another direction. Make love your aim, your goal, and your response. Let love shape your character, refine your motives, and guide your actions. Over time, love will become not just something you do, but who you are. When you commit to walking in love daily, you become a vessel of peace in a restless world, a light in moments of darkness, and a living testimony of grace in action. Love changes atmospheres, heals relationships, and reflects the heart of God to everyone it touches. Commit yourself today to walk in love. Give yourself to it. Pursue it. Let love lead the way.

John 13:35 says, "By this everyone will know that you are My disciples, if you love one another." Love is our distinct calling for it is the evidence that we belong to God. Among all virtues, gifts, and callings, love stands as the unmistakable trait that sets us apart. It is the unmistakable mark of a life genuinely transformed by God. Scripture does not present love as optional or conditional, but as the very essence of our calling. To love is not simply good behavior - it is our obedience to the heart of God and alignment with His nature. God commands us to love one another as He loves us. This command sets the standard far beyond human affection, convenience, or preference. God's love is sacrificial, patient, faithful, and relentless.

He loves without reservation and gives without counting the cost. When He calls us to love as He loves, He is calling us into a higher way of living - one that reflects heaven on earth and reveals His character to a watching world. Love distinguishes us. It's what makes us different.

Titles, knowledge, accomplishments, and spiritual activity mean little if love is absent. Love is what makes our faith visible and credible. Jesus made it clear that love would be the identifying mark of His followers - not power, not influence, not even zeal, but love. When we love as He loves, we bear unmistakable witness that God is alive within us. This calling to love reaches beyond comfort and convenience. It calls us to love when it is difficult, to forgive when we have been wronged, to show kindness when it is undeserved, and to extend grace when it costs us something. God's love is not passive; it moves toward people in their brokenness, weakness, and need. In the same way, we are called to pursue others with compassion, humility, and mercy. Loving as God loves means choosing patience over irritation, forgiveness over resentment, and humility over pride. It means refusing to let offense, bitterness, or fear take the throne where faith, peace, and obedience to God belong.

Love requires intentionality. It must be chosen daily, protected diligently, and practiced consistently. It is a decision to place the well-being of others above self-interest and to reflect God's heart in every relationship. This love is not produced by human strength alone. It flows from abiding in God. As we remain close to Him, His love fills us and overflows through us.

The more we receive His love, the more freely we can give it. God never commands us to do what He does not empower us to accomplish. His Spirit enables us to love beyond our natural limits and to walk in love even when our emotions resist. Love is our highest calling because it is eternal. Faith and hope are essential, but love outlasts them all. To walk in love is to walk in obedience. To live in love is to live in alignment with God's purpose. Love shapes our character, strengthens our witness, and leaves a lasting impact on the lives of others. When everything else fades, love remains. Every act of love echoes into eternity.

When we commit ourselves to love one another as God has loved us, we step into a calling that is both holy and costly. This kind of love is not rooted in emotion alone, nor is it dependent on convenience, agreement, or reward. It is a deliberate choice to reflect the nature of God Himself - a love that reaches first, forgives freely, and gives sacrificially. To love as God loves is to allow His character to shape our attitudes, our words, and our actions, even when doing so stretches us beyond our comfort. God's love is patient with our weaknesses and faithful in our failures. It is a love that does not abandon us when we fall short but instead draws us closer and restores us. When we commit to loving one another in this same way, we become living expressions of grace. We learn to see people not merely as they are, but as God sees them - valuable, and worthy of compassion. This transforms relationships, families, churches, and communities, because love has the power to heal what bitterness has broken.

Loving as Christ loved also means embracing humility. Jesus did not love from a distance; He entered our brokenness, carried our burdens, and served with His life. When we follow His example, love moves beyond words into action. It listens before it speaks, serves without seeking recognition, and chooses reconciliation over resentment. This kind of love resists the urge to keep score and instead seeks unity, knowing that true strength is found in self-giving rather than self-protection. Our distinct calling as believers is not merely to speak about Christ, but to reflect His heart through the way we treat one another. Love becomes our testimony. In a world marked by division, fear, and self-interest, Christlike love stands as a powerful witness of God's kingdom. It shows that the gospel is not only true, but transformative. When people encounter genuine love, they encounter the presence of God at work in His people.

Ultimately, committing ourselves to love one another as God has loved us shapes us into who we were created to be. This kind of love refines our hearts, aligns our actions with God's purpose, and moves us beyond selfish living. When we choose love daily, we reflect the character of Christ in both word and deed. In loving others faithfully, we step fully into our calling and reveal the image of God within us. Love draws our hearts into alignment with heaven, tuning our desires to what is holy, pure, and eternal. It becomes the anchor of our lives, steadying us when the storms of this world try to pull us off course. Rooted in love, we discover an eternal purpose that reaches beyond the present and reflects the very heart of God. As we walk in this love each day - choosing patience, extending mercy, and offering grace - we reflect the very heart of Christ in a world desperate for truth and compassion. In doing so, we fulfill our calling and draw others toward the hope, healing, and redemption that are found in Him alone.

Love is not merely an emotion, a sentiment, or a fleeting feeling. In the kingdom of God, love is evidence. It is the unmistakable, visible mark that separates those who claim they know Christ from those who truly follow Him. Jesus Himself declared that love - not gifts, not knowledge, not power—would be the distinguishing mark of all who call Him Lord. Christianity is not proven by what we say, how much Scripture we can quote, or how passionately we worship. It is proven by how we love. Love is not an accessory to the Christian life; it is its very foundation, shaping how we think, speak, and live each day. When love leads, our faith becomes visible, authentic, and powerful - reflecting Christ in every relationship and response. Remove love, and what remains may still look religious, filled with rituals, words, and outward form, but it is hollow and powerless. True faith is proven not by appearance or activity, but by love that reflects the heart, character, and transforming power of Christ.

The apostle Paul made this unmistakably clear when he wrote that without love, even the most impressive spiritual achievements amount to nothing. One can speak with eloquence, possess great faith, understand deep mysteries, and perform sacrificial acts yet still miss the heart of God if love is absent. Love is the atmosphere of heaven where every thought, word, and action flows from the heart of God. As we walk in love here on earth, we align our lives with heaven's culture and allow others to experience a glimpse of eternity through us. Love is the language of the Kingdom spoken through humility, compassion, and selfless action rather than mere words. When we choose to love as Christ loves, we communicate heaven's values to the world and reveal the true power and presence of God at work within us. Love is the nature of God Himself, the essence of who He is. Everything He does flows from this perfect love, revealing His heart, His will, and His desire to redeem and restore.

God does not merely show love - He is love. Therefore, to follow Him is to reflect His nature. A loveless Christian is a contradiction, just as a dark light or dry water would be. Biblical love is not driven by emotion; it is driven by obedience. Love is a decision - one that must be made daily, often moment by moment. Jesus loved intentionally. He loved deliberately. He loved sacrificially. He loved the overlooked, He touched the untouchable, He welcomed the rejected, He forgave the guilty, He served the ungrateful, He prayed for His enemies. This was not weakness - it was divine strength. Spiritual maturity is not measured by how much we know, but by how well we love. Immaturity reacts, love responds. Immaturity insists on being right, love seeks to be righteous. Immaturity tears down, love builds up. When love governs our actions, it produces unity instead of division, healing instead of harm, and peace instead of conflict. Love does not ignore truth but it delivers truth with grace.

If love is the defining mark of the follower of Christ, then every man must ask an honest question, "What mark am I leaving on the world?" Are our words marked by love? Are our actions marked by love? Are our relationships marked by love? Are our responses marked by love? Love is not weakness - it is the strongest force on earth, powerful enough to heal wounds, conquer fear, and transform lives. True strength is revealed not in domination or hardness, but in the courage to love selflessly, sacrificially, and without condition. Love transforms hardened hearts, shatters the chains of sin, fear, and shame, and brings freedom where bondage once ruled. When love is lived out through us, it reveals Jesus clearly to a watching world as the power that redeems, heals, and makes all things new. When love takes the lead, Christ is clearly revealed through our words, actions, and attitudes. And when Christ is seen, hearts are transformed, chains are broken, and lives are forever changed.

To call Jesus Lord is to commit to living His way, choosing to walk where He leads, even when the path is narrow, costly, or countercultural. Jesus made His way unmistakably clear: His way is love. Not a shallow or conditional love, but a sacrificial, self-giving love that seeks the good of others above self. It is the kind of love that forgives when wronged, serves when unnoticed, and remains faithful when it would be easier to walk away. Love is not an accessory to the Christian life but is the defining evidence that Christ truly reigns in us. To live His way is to let love shape our words, guide our decisions, and govern our relationships. It is choosing compassion over convenience, humility over pride, and grace over retaliation. When love leads, Christ is revealed, and the world is changed. To call Jesus Lord is to commit to living His way and His way will always be love. May we be men who are unmistakably marked by love. Because love is, and always will be, the distinguishing mark of all who truly follow Jesus.

| 19 |

"EFFECTIVE MINISTRY"

The greatest need in the church today is a fresh filling and outpouring of faith, hope, and love. Faith that once trusted God boldly must be renewed, not as mere belief, but as confident obedience that expects Him to move again. When faith is alive, the church no longer shrinks back in fear or compromise, but stands firmly convinced that God is still able, still willing, and still working. Along with faith, the church desperately needs a renewed outpouring of hope. Many hearts have grown weary from prolonged trials, cultural pressure, and delayed promises. Biblical hope is not wishful thinking; it is an anchored assurance that God's purposes will prevail. When hope is restored, the church lifts its eyes beyond present struggles and lives with courage, endurance, and joyful expectation of what God is bringing forth. Above all, there must be a fresh filling of the love of Christ flowing through His people. When love is poured out, the church becomes a living witness of Jesus to a hurting world.

Love heals wounds, restores unity, and draws the lost to Christ, proving that the power of God is not only seen in what we believe, but in how we live and love one another. When we are filled with the love of God, something within us changes. His love reshapes our hearts, renews our minds, and gives us a strength that does not come from circumstances. In a world often marked by fear, division, and confusion, God's love anchors us in truth and peace. It reminds us of who we are and whose we are, empowering us to live with confidence, compassion, and purpose. The love of God does not stay hidden inside us; it naturally shines outward. Just as light cannot be concealed in darkness, His love, expressed through our words, attitudes, and actions, becomes a living testimony that others can see and experience. When we walk in love consistently, we reveal the heart of God. People may not understand our faith, but they cannot deny the light they see shining through a life transformed by His love.

As we walk daily in the love of God, we become beacons of hope in a dark world. Our lives point others toward the source of true light - Jesus Christ - who calls us to shine before others so they may see His goodness. When we allow God's love to fill us completely, we do more than survive the darkness around us; we overcome it. His love shining through us becomes an invitation for others to step out of the shadows and into the light of His grace. When the light of Christ fills our innermost being, it cannot be hidden. It radiates through our words, our tone, and our actions, quietly declaring hope where despair once ruled. This light is not manufactured by effort or performance; it is the natural overflow of a heart surrendered to God and transformed by His presence. Those living in darkness are often not drawn by arguments or forceful persuasion, but by the gentle contrast of light. In a world weighed down by fear, confusion, and brokenness, a life marked by peace, integrity, and love stands out.

The light within us exposes nothing harshly. Instead, it invites, warms, and offers a glimpse of something better. As that light shines, it creates a hunger in others for what they see but may not yet understand. People begin to notice the steadiness in our trials, the compassion in our responses, and the joy that remains even in hardship. This visible difference awakens questions in the hearts of those searching for meaning beyond the darkness they know. When we remain faithful to walk in the light God has given us, our lives begin to shine with a steady, unmistakable glow. Through that faithful walk, God uses us as living beacons quietly yet powerfully guiding others toward Him and His truth. Without striving for attention, the light radiating from within us becomes a living pathway, guiding those who walk in darkness toward hope, life, and true freedom. When Christ shines through our words, actions, and character, others are drawn not to us but to the transforming power of Christ alone.

Love is the heartbeat of effective ministry, because without it our words become noise and our actions lose their power. Genuine love reflects the character of Christ, opening hearts that teaching alone can never reach. When love leads, ministry moves beyond duty and becomes a life-giving expression of God's grace to others. In 1 Cor. 13:1-3 Paul identifies six gifts that are given to Christian believers. He speaks about eloquent speech, spiritual experiences, brilliant minds, outstanding achievements, unusual generosity, and courageous commitment. These are all marvelous gifts from the hand of God and love is needed to effectively operate in these gifts. Nothing is gained when we operate in our gift without love, because ability without compassion produces noise, not impact. Gifts may impress people, but love is what transforms lives and honors God. When love leads our gift, what we do carries eternal weight and lasting fruit. We must all grow in love because love is essential for effective ministry.

Let pursuing love be the highest priority of your life, because love is not an accessory to faith - it is its very essence. Scripture reminds us that without love, even the greatest gifts, achievements, and sacrifices amount to nothing. You can possess knowledge, strength, influence, and faith that moves mountains, but if love does not guide your heart, those things lose their eternal value. Love is what gives meaning to obedience and purpose to every calling God places on your life. When love becomes your pursuit, it reshapes how you see people and how you respond to life. Love teaches patience when you want to react, kindness when you are tempted to withdraw, and humility when pride seeks control. It anchors your actions in grace rather than ego and turns daily interactions into opportunities to reflect God's heart. A life driven by love does not seek applause or recognition; it seeks to build, heal, and restore. In the end, love is the measure by which everything else will be weighed.

Titles will fade, accomplishments will be forgotten, and possessions will pass away but love endures forever. Make it your aim to love God wholeheartedly and to love others intentionally, because this is the legacy that lasts. When love is your priority, your life will speak with power, authenticity, and eternal significance. Daily let your love for others be deepened, refreshed, and renewed. Go out of your way and do something nice for them. Ask God to enlarge your heart so you may grow deeper in love for your family, your fellow brethren, and those who have not yet given their lives to Christ. As His love fills you, let it flow through you with grace, patience, and compassion, becoming a living witness of Christ to all. Act like a man and ask God to help you meet the needs of those around you. Ask Him to let you be the answer to their prayers. Take the initiative by opening your eyes to unmet needs, because leaders actively look for problems so they can bring solutions, growth, and lasting impact.

Love is the foundation of all effective ministry. That's why Paul said to let all you do be done in love. In 1 Cor. 13, Paul lists several ways in which walking in love will change you and equip you for life. Vs. 4-7 says, "Love is patient and kind; love does not envy; love does not parade itself, is not puffed up; does not behave rudely, does not seek its own, is not provoked, thinks no evil; does not rejoice in iniquity, but rejoices in the truth; bears all things, believes all things, hopes all thing, endures all things." Like a well-groomed tree, love bears fruit in every area of life, strengthening relationships, purpose, and character. The more you grow in love, the more you flourish—spreading life, shade, and blessing to everyone around you. Love is the supreme gift from God, poured into our hearts with divine purpose and eternal value. When embraced and lived out daily, it produces marvelous fruit—transforming our character, strengthening our relationships, and leaving a lasting legacy of faith and compassion.

What does love do? First of all, "love suffers long and is kind" (1 Cor. 13:4). Love places a holy restraint on the evil impulses of the flesh, governing your reactions when your natural instinct is to retaliate. It empowers you to turn the other cheek, choosing grace over revenge when others do you wrong. In doing so, love reflects the heart of Christ and transforms conflict into a testimony of strength and spiritual maturity. 1 Peter 3:9 (NLT), "Don't repay evil for evil. Don't retaliate with insults when people insult you. Instead, pay them back with a blessing. This is what God has called you to do, and He will bless you for it." The Message Bible says, "No retaliation. No sharp-tongued sarcasm. Instead, bless. That's your job, to bless." Peter calls us to rise above retaliation and refuse the instinct to repay wrong with more wrong. When insults come, God invites us to respond not from wounded pride, but from transformed hearts. Choosing to bless instead of strike back reflects Christ's character at work within us.

Love does not envy (vs. 4). When you grow in love, your heart matures beyond possession and comparison, finding joy in another's blessing even when it looks like something you wanted for yourself. True love celebrates God's goodness in others, trusting that what is meant for you will come in His time. You'll celebrate when your co-worker gets that promotion even though you were more qualified and better equipped for the position. You'll be happy when your neighbor comes home with a new car when you've been believing for one for months. You may not think these people deserved what they received but you rejoice with them anyway. Why? Because love does not envy. Love delivers you from the self-destructive power of envy by shifting your focus from comparison to compassion. When love governs your heart, another person's blessing inspires gratitude and hope. Instead of resenting what others receive, love empowers you to rejoice, knowing that a generous God has more than enough for all.

"Love does not boast; it is not arrogant" (vs. 4). Envy focuses on what others have; pride focuses on what you have. Love is God's antidote to pride and arrogance because it redirects the heart from self-exaltation to Christlike surrender. It does not parade itself or seek recognition but quietly serves with sincerity and obedience. When love governs your life, it produces the good fruit of humility, shaping a spirit that honors God and lifts others above self. "Love is not rude. It does not act becomingly, does not behave itself unseemly. It does not insist on its own way" (vs. 5). Love does not behave inappropriately; it chooses honor over impulse and respect over self-gratification. It is mindful of words, attitudes, and actions, understanding that careless behavior can wound hearts and leave lasting scars. True love walks gently, intentionally guarding the feelings of others and seeking to build, not bruise. It is attentive to the courtesies of life. It never speaks in a way that is insensitive to the feelings of others.

Love equips you to speak the right words at the right time. It gives you discernment to know what to say, how to say it, and when silence or speech will bring the greatest good. When love leads, your words carry truth, grace, and life exactly when they are needed most. Love stretches your heart beyond self, sharpening emotional intelligence by teaching patience, empathy, and understanding. When love leads, it equips you to build, sustain, and protect healthy relationships that grow stronger over time. Walking in love will enable you to behave and speak appropriately. You'll be sensitive to how others will respond to what you say and do to them. Love gives you a deep self-assurance because it makes you mindful of how your words and actions shape the hearts and lives of others. When you walk in love, you move with confidence, knowing your influence is guided by care, purpose, and responsibility. It will cause you to be more considerate, diplomatic, and thoughtful in your interactions with other people.

"Love is not irritable or resentful. It is not easily provoked; thinks no evil" (vs. 5). When someone deliberately provokes or annoys you, it's easy and natural to assume the worst about their motives and character. But wisdom calls us to pause, guard our thoughts, and choose grace because reacting in love reveals strength, maturity, and godly self-control. Love chooses grace over suspicion and looks for the good before assuming the bad. It gives others the benefit of the doubt, even when circumstances invite misunderstanding. Rather than reacting to flaws, love responds with patience, humility, and mercy. In doing so, love protects relationships and reflects the heart of Christ. Love will always make the most generous judgment possible. It chooses grace over suspicion and seeks understanding before forming conclusions. It looks beyond faults, believing the best and offering mercy where others might withhold it. Love will give them the benefit of the doubt before it ever assumes the worst.

"Love does not rejoice in wrongdoing but rejoices with the truth" (vs. 6). Love does not celebrate what is wrong, even when it benefits us or feels justified in the moment. It refuses to take pleasure in sin, deception, or another person's failure. Instead, love finds its joy in what is true, pure, and right before God. When truth prevails, love rejoices because truth always leads to freedom, healing, and life. Phil. 1:9, "And this I pray, that your love may abound still more and more in knowledge and all discernment." Love is not meant to remain shallow or stagnant, but to grow continually deeper and stronger. As our love abounds more and more, it is to be guided by knowledge and sharpened by discernment, so it reflects God's wisdom and truth. This kind of love learns, chooses wisely, and acts intentionally for the good of others and the glory of God. The more you walk in love, the more you'll know what is good and true and righteous. You'll be drawn to these good things and will find joy in it.

Vs. 7 says love "bears all things, believes all things, hopes all things, endures all things." The Message Bible says love "puts up with anything, trusts God always, always looks for the best, never looks back, but keeps going to the end." Walk in love, and you will find the strength to carry every burden placed on your shoulders. Love does not remove the weight, but it gives you the grace, endurance, and peace to bear it well. Walk in love, and you create an atmosphere where trust can grow naturally. When your words and actions are rooted in genuine love, relationships are strengthened by honesty, safety, and lasting confidence. Walk in love, and you will always carry a living hope within you, even when the world around you grows dark. Love anchors your heart in God's promises, giving light, strength, and confidence that no circumstance can extinguish. Walk in love, and you will always find the strength to endure, no matter how hard or heavy the circumstances become.

Love will equip you for life, giving you the strength, wisdom, and grace to face every season with purpose. It is a gift of supreme value, shaping your character and empowering you to impact others in ways nothing else can. Every day, seek to grow in love, for as love increases, so does the depth and meaning of your life. Always remember that walking in love is a command from God, not a suggestion or an option. Love is the evidence of true obedience and the mark of a life submitted to His will. When you walk in love, you are answering your calling from above and reflecting the heart of Christ to the world. 1 John 4:21, "And this commandment we have from Him: whoever loves God must also love His brother." Ask God to help you grow in love, because love does not come naturally to the flesh but is formed through surrender and obedience. 1 Thess. 3:12, "May the Lord make you increase and abound in love for one another." As you walk with Him daily, He shapes your heart to love as He loves.

When you are born again, the Holy Spirit comes to dwell within you, bringing with Him the very presence of God. With God's presence comes God's love, poured into your heart and made real in your daily life. This means every true Christian believer carries the love of God within, not as a feeling alone, but as a living reality meant to be expressed. God pours His love into your heart through the Holy Spirit, filling you with a love that originates in Him and never runs dry. It is from this divine love within you that you are empowered to genuinely love others as He loves you. Never think you are incapable of showing great love. His love flows to you so it can flow through you, touching others with the same grace and power you have received. Be intentional in your walk of love, choosing each day to reflect patience, kindness, and grace in every interaction. Let love be your conscious purpose - guiding your words, shaping your actions, and defining the legacy you leave behind.

2 Peter 1:5-7, "Make every effort to supplement your faith with goodness, and goodness with brotherly affection, and brother affection with love." Always seek the good of others, choosing love over convenience and service over self. Put their interests above your own, not because it is easy, but because it reflects Christlike character and strength. Do this intentionally knowing that what you sow into others will shape your legacy. Your calling is to become a living channel through which God's love reaches others, not by your own strength, but through your willing heart. When you surrender yourself to that purpose, you discover that loving others becomes an act of divine partnership, not personal pressure. Find deep joy in this sacred

privilege, because letting God love others through you is one of the highest honors of your calling. His love is perfected in you and accomplishes its intended purpose. When you love others, God's love is seen and made known. That's what being a man is all about.

| 20 |

"AN HONEST MAN"

The best, the deepest, and the closet friend you can ever be is to love someone enough that you'll speak the truth to them in love. It's when you value their growth more than your comfort and their destiny more than your approval. True friendship is proven when honesty is given with grace, compassion, and a sincere desire for someone's good and well-being. Sometimes love speaks uncomfortable truth - the kind others avoid because it costs too much to say. You'll tell people things about their life that no one else cared enough to speak, not to wound them, but to wake them. And yes, it may put the friendship on the line, but real love risks loss so growth can be gained. If truly listened to, the words you speak have the power to interrupt a dangerous path and redirect a friend's life toward purpose and truth. One honest conversation, spoken in love and courage, can become the turning point that changes their future forever. We don't judge people, but we are called to speak the truth to them in love.

Rom. 15:14 (ESV), "You are full of goodness, filled with all knowledge and able to instruct one another." The Message Bible says, "You seem to me to be well-motivated and well-instructed, quite capable of guiding and advising one another." Because you care, you don't stay silent - you go to them in love, not to condemn but to restore, gently pointing out the places in their life that don't line up with the Word of God. True love isn't afraid of truth; it is willing to have the hard conversation so healing, growth, and alignment can take place. When correction is wrapped in compassion and guided by Scripture, it becomes an act of faithfulness that helps a person walk closer to who God has called them to be The King James Bible says we must be "able also to admonish one another." The word "admonish" means 'to exert influence upon another by life and words, to guide into obedience of God's will as revealed in scripture.' The Greek word for "admonish" is "noutheteo" and it means literally 'to place in the mind.'

Paul had to confront the Corinthians with some hard truths. He calls them his dear brothers and sisters because he wants his affection for them to be clear. He wants them to know he cares about them and, because he cares, he's going to say some hard truths to them. 1 Cor. 4:14 says, "I do not write these things to shame you, but as my beloved children I warn you." He is a watchman on the wall, eyes fixed on the horizon, heart burdened with love for those below. He does not cry out to frighten them, but to protect them, for he sees what others cannot yet see - the enemy drawing near. His warning is not condemnation but compassion, not anger but concern. Because he loves them, he refuses to be silent; because he cares, he lifts his voice while there is still time to prepare, to turn, and to stand ready. His call is an act of mercy, a final kindness before the battle reaches the gates, urging them to wake up, take heed, and find safety while it can still be found.

Silence in the face of spiritual danger is not kindness - it is neglect. Not saying anything because you don't want to hurt someone's feelings may feel compassionate, but in truth it is equivalent to spiritual malpractice. Love does not ignore truth; it speaks it with courage and care. When someone is walking toward harm, remaining quiet to preserve comfort is choosing temporary peace over eternal good. True love is willing to risk misunderstanding, discomfort, and even rejection if it means protecting a soul from deeper damage. It is no different than a doctor who sees a deadly spot on a patient's lung but refuses to speak up because the news might be upsetting. Instead of diagnosing the problem and prescribing the cure, he masks the pain with morphine and asks the patient to return later. That isn't mercy - it's malpractice. In the same way, offering soothing words while withholding truth may ease emotions for a moment, but it allows the disease to grow. Real care confronts the issue and points to the remedy.

Saving a life matters more than sparing feelings. As a real man you must be committed to doing the right thing even if it's uncomfortable. Paul said, "Night and day for a period of three years I did not cease to admonish each one with tears (Acts 20:31). If you see something wrong in somebody's life and don't say anything, you're responsible for what happens to them. Ezek. 33:6, "If the watchman sees the enemy coming and doesn't sound the alarm to warn the people, he is responsible for their captivity." God is calling all men to be watchmen for one another, remaining spiritually alert and deeply invested in the lives of our brothers. A watchman does not stay silent when danger approaches, because love demands action. Speaking the truth in love is not about judgment, but about restoration, and growth. It calls for humility, courage, and a heart committed to restoration instead of taking offense. When men courageously combine truth with compassion, they help guard hearts, strengthen faith, and honor God.

A real man is an honest man. He doesn't hide behind silence or pretend that everything is fine when it clearly isn't. True strength is found in the courage to confront what's wrong with humility and love. Speaking the truth in love may feel risky, because honesty can be misunderstood or resisted. Yet remaining silent carries a far greater cost - the loss of growth, healing, and alignment with what is right. One man saw a married friend of his flirting with another woman. He knew he should have said something but didn't. A few months later this friend left his wife for the other woman, bringing pain and heartache to all his family. Speaking the truth in love to this man may have set him on a different path than the one he had taken. So yes, saying nothing was the wrong thing to do. According to Ezekiel, this man who said nothing is responsible for the divorce between his friend and his wife. When truth is withheld, opportunities for change fade, but when it is spoken in love, it can bring life, clarity, and freedom.

When something weighs heavy on his heart, a real doesn't gossip, avoid, or harden himself - he goes directly to the person involved. He speaks truth not to wound, but to restore; not to elevate himself, but to help another see what they may be too close, too hurt, or too proud to recognize. This kind of honesty requires bravery, compassion, and integrity, because it risks misunderstanding for the sake of growth. A real man chooses truth over comfort, clarity over avoidance, and love over fear, even when the conversation is difficult. Act like a man by standing firm in your values, taking responsibility, and choosing faithfulness over comfort. True commitment is proven when you walk alongside others, helping them rise, heal, and move forward on their journey through life. Speak the truth in love. "Encourage one another and build each other up" (1 Thess. 5:11). Eph. 4:29, "Speak only what is helpful for building others up according to their needs, that it may benefit those who listen."

You don't bring positive change by tearing people down and being critical of them. This is what draws them away from God, not to Him. You're to be honest but don't be brutally honest. You're not there to tear down but to build up. You're there to speak the truth in love, not to win an argument but to help bring light and growth. Let the tone of your voice reflect the love in your heart, so your words heal rather than wound. When truth is spoken with genuine care, it has the power to guide, restore, and strengthen others on their journey. Paul wrote in 2 Cor. 2:4 concerning the first letter he sent to them, "I wrote that letter in great anguish, with a troubled heart and many tears. I didn't want to grieve you, but I wanted to let you know how much love I have for you." The admonition he confronted them with was written with a heavy heart, each word shaped by deep concern rather than judgment. Tears flowed down his face as he spoke the truth in love, longing not to wound them, but to call them back to what was right.

Col. 4:6, "Let your conversation be gracious and attractive so that you will have the right response for everyone." When you must correct or admonish someone, let kindness lead the way so your words heal rather than wound. Speak the truth in love, remembering that grace and humility give truth its power to be received. Correction offered with a gentle heart reflects the very nature of Christ - full of grace, truth, and love. Jesus never corrected to shame or crush, but to restore, heal, and guide hearts back to what is right. When correction is wrapped in humility and compassion, it becomes a tool for growth rather than a weapon of harm. A gentle approach preserves dignity, invites understanding, and opens the door for repentance and transformation. Instead of tearing others down, Christlike correction builds them up, strengthening faith, deepening relationships, and fostering unity. In this way, correction becomes an expression of love - one that seeks restoration and reflects the heart of Christ in both word and spirit.

Paul later tells the results that came from his words of encouragement spoken to the church at Corinth. 2 Cor. 7:8-10 (MSG) says, "I know I distressed you greatly with my letter. Although I felt awful at the time, I don't feel at all bad now that I see how it turned out. Now I'm glad, not that you were upset, but that you were jarred into turning things around. You let the distress bring you to God, not drive you from Him. The result was all gain, no loss. Distress that drives us to God does that. It turns us around. It gets us back in the way of salvation. We never regret that kind of pain." Repentance is not God humiliating us; it is God rescuing us. When godly sorrow enters the heart, it produces a turning - not just from sin, but toward righteousness. It realigns our desires, reshapes our priorities, and restores intimacy with God. There is no regret in this kind of repentance. When we respond rightly to conviction, sorrow becomes a sacred doorway leading us out of compromise and into renewed fellowship with God.

To admonish one another is an act of love that combines encouragement, wise counsel, and timely warning. It calls us to speak truth with humility, helping others see both the direction they are heading and the consequences of their choices. When done with compassion, admonition strengthens character, restores relationships, and guides hearts back toward what is right. In short, the Greek word "noutheteo" refers to giving loving counsel that includes a clear warning, not to condemn but to protect and guide. It identifies a spiritual obstacle that must be confronted, removed, or changed in order to walk in truth and growth. It seeks to correct the mind by renewing our thoughts with truth, making right what has been twisted or led astray. In doing so, it reshapes the heart and improves one's spiritual attitude, aligning the soul with God's will and purpose. Theologian A. T. Robertson says it means "putting sense into the heads of people. A thankless, but necessary task."

Admonishment, when given in truth and love, is a critically important function that preserves the vitality, unity, and spiritual health of the body of Christ by guiding believers back to God's will. To admonish means to express warning or disapproval to someone in a gentle and earnest manner. To reprove firmly but not harshly means to speak truth with courage while guarding the heart of compassion. Correction is not meant to crush or shame, but to guide someone back toward what is right. When love is the motive, admonishment becomes an act of care, seeking restoration rather than condemnation. Gal. 6:1, "If anyone is caught in any trespass, you who are spiritual, restore such a one in a spirit of gentleness." 1 Thess. 5:14, "We urge you, brethren, admonish the unruly, encourage the fainthearted, help the weak, be patient with everyone." Col. 1:28, "We proclaim Him, admonishing every man and teaching every man with all wisdom, so that we may present every man perfect in Christ."

The willingness and ability to admonish others is a clear mark of spiritual maturity, because it reflects a heart that values truth, love, and growth over comfort or avoidance. As we grow up in Christ, we move beyond a shallow faith that only receives instruction and step into a mature faith that can lovingly give it. Spiritual maturity produces discernment, humility, and courage - discernment to recognize when correction is needed, humility to speak from a place of love rather than superiority, and courage to address issues for the sake of restoration. Admonition, when rooted in Christlike love, is not about condemnation but edification, helping one another walk more faithfully in obedience to God. In this way, growing in Christ equips us to instruct one another, strengthening the body of believers and fostering unity, accountability, and spiritual health. Act like a man. Care about people and be willing to confront them when they've gotten off the path they're supposed to be on.

Admonishing consists of reminding, warning, counseling, correcting, reproving, and rebuking a person with the intention that they will carry it out. Admonition is not judgment. It's caring enough to be willing to confront a person in a spirit of love and compassion. Admonishment is not spoken with casual words. It speaks specifically about a specific area where the person is clearly out of God's will. It implies a definite and specific exhortation, correction, and warning to lead the person to a specific action. You don't speak down to a person you're admonishing. It is equal to equal, brother to brother, saved sinner to saved sinner. Be sensitive to God's Spirit and the lives of others. Don't leave things the way they are because you fear rejection. Admonishment is personal in nature and directed toward a specific individual. Don't speak to a crowd and hope the person catches your meaning. It may not be enjoyable to admonish another person, but it is the most loving thing you could ever do.

Some people may not be aware that what they're doing is wrong because their actions have been shaped by habit, culture, or past experiences rather than thoughtful reflection. David prayed, "Cleanse me from secret faults" (Ps. 19:12). CEV, "Forgive me when I sin without knowing it." NET, "Please do not punish me for sins I am unaware of." When a behavior becomes normal in someone's environment, it can feel justified or even harmless, especially if it has never been challenged. In many cases, ignorance is not intentional but the result of limited understanding, emotional blindness, or an avoidance of accountability. People often act from what they know, and if their knowledge is incomplete or distorted, their choices will reflect that. Growth begins when awareness is introduced when truth, empathy, and perspective gently reveal what was once unseen and open the door to change. There will be times when God will use you to point out hidden sins to a brother. It's called admonishment.

Doing this is not a one-time action but a continual commitment that demands consistency. To truly be effective, it must be pursued with persistence, growing stronger and more intentional over time. What begins as discipline must mature into a relentless resolve that refuses to quit. 1 Thess. 2:12 (NLT), "We pleaded with you, encouraged you, and urged you to live your lives in a way that God would consider worthy." The Message Bible says, "With each of you we were like a father with his child, holding your hand, whispering encouragement, showing you step-by-step how to live well before God." The true test of love is not patting people on the back telling them how wonderful they are, but the courage to speak truth, challenge growth, and seek what is best for someone even when it's uncomfortable. It's wanting what's best for them so bad that you're willing to risk the relationship by admonishing them. Speaking the truth in love will show the other person you care for them and are not judging them.

1 Cor. 16:13,14 says you are to "act like men" and 'let all that you do be done in love." This is the agape love of God, a self-sacrificial love that seeks the highest good of the one loved, not its own advantage. It gives without demanding, serves without keeping score, and remains faithful even when unreturned. This love moves beyond emotion into action, willingly laying itself down for another's benefit. Agape love transforms lives because it reflects the very heart and nature of God. Speak truth with the purpose of strengthening and building others up, not tearing them down. Let every word you share bring encouragement, clarity, and benefit to the one who hears it. Eph. 4:29, "Let no corrupt communication come out of your mouth, but what is good for necessary edification, that it may impart grace to the hearer." Before you speak, pause and ask whether your words are true, helpful, inspiring, necessary, and kind because speech guided by wisdom builds life, not regret.

Speaking the truth in love requires discernment, because even sincere words can fall on closed hearts. If someone is not ready to receive correction or wisdom, truth may sound like rejection instead of care. Love waits for the right moment, trusting God to prepare the heart before the message is spoken. When you act like a man, you learn that strength isn't measured by volume or bravado, but by wisdom, restraint, and clarity. It's not just what you say that carries weight - it's how you say it, because the right tone reveals character, confidence, and maturity. God has called all men to love one another and help one another. He wants men to speak into each other's lives. Speaking the truth in love is an act of courage. It takes real courage to do the will of God - standing firm to do what is right and to speak truth even when it costs you. It's not easy but, when all is said and done, the person you're admonishing will be better off than they were before. That's the goal, isn't it?

| 21 |

"MEN WITH INTEGRITY"

David asked in Ps. 15:1, "Lord, who may abide in Your tabernacle? Who may dwell in Your holy hill?" In other words, who can experience the goodness and the presence and the peace of God? He then answers his own question in vs. 2,3, "Those who lead blameless lives and do what is right, speaking the truth from sincere hearts. Those who refuse to gossip or harm their neighbors or speak evil of their friends." He's talking about those who live and walk with integrity. These are the ones who dwell in the presence of the Lord. He says in vs. 6 that whoever walks uprightly in the fear of the Lord will not be shaken. Those who walk with integrity will be strong and will always walk in love. A rich person lost a wallet with a huge sum of money in it. A passerby found it and returned it to the owner. Everybody was shocked by this good deed. They couldn't believe the guy returned so much money. It is tragic that we live in a world where people are more shocked by integrity than they are by a lack of integrity.

Integrity is not a trait a man of God turns on when it is convenient, nor is it a public image he wears to impress others. Integrity is who he is when no one is watching, when the applause is gone, and when compromise would be easier than obedience. A man of God is called to walk in integrity at all times not because it is comfortable, but because it is faithful. Integrity is the alignment of belief, speech, and action under the authority of God. It is living the same life in private that one claims in public. The Scriptures teach that "the integrity of the upright shall guide them" (Prov. 11:3). Integrity is not merely a moral option; it is a guiding force. Without it, a man may possess talent, strength, or influence, but he will lack trustworthiness and, without trust, leadership collapses. A man of God understands that integrity begins in the heart. Long before actions are visible, motives are formed. God does not only judge outward behavior; He weighs the intentions of the heart.

Charles Colson, "The three most important ingredients in Christian work is integrity, integrity, integrity." A man may fool people, but he cannot fool God. Integrity requires a man to allow the Word of God to search him, correct him, and cleanse him. It demands humility - the willingness to be honest with God about weaknesses, temptations, and failures. Integrity is not sinlessness; it is sincerity. When a man of God falls, integrity moves him to repentance, not excuses. Walking in integrity means choosing obedience over convenience. The world rewards shortcuts, half-truths, and silent compromise. But a man of God understands that obedience to God often costs something. It may cost popularity, profit, position, or comfort. Yet integrity refuses to trade eternal reward for temporary gain. Like Joseph, who fled temptation rather than entertain it, a man of God values a clear conscience more than momentary pleasure. He would rather suffer for doing right than succeed by doing wrong.

Integrity governs a man's words. A man of God speaks truth even when truth is uncomfortable. He does not manipulate language to deceive, exaggerate, or protect his ego. His yes means yes, and his no means no. He understands that words carry weight - that careless speech can destroy trust built over years. A man of integrity does not flatter to gain favor, nor does he speak harshly to assert dominance. His speech is seasoned with truth, wisdom, and grace. Integrity also shapes a man's relationships. A man of God treats others with fairness, honor, and respect. He does not exploit people for personal gain or use relationships as steppingstones. He remains faithful in his marriage, loyal in friendship, and honorable in leadership. A man of God does not live a divided life - one for church and one for the world - but a unified life surrendered fully to God. John MacArthur, "A person with integrity is one whose thoughts, beliefs, words, and actions are all in perfect harmony."

Shakespeare said, "What stronger breastplate than a heart untainted." Walking in integrity requires courage. It takes courage to stand alone when others choose compromise. It takes courage to admit fault when pride demands self-defense. It takes courage to do what is right when no one would know if you did otherwise. Integrity is proven in pressure. When temptation intensifies and consequences loom, integrity anchors a man to truth rather than emotion. It is easy to talk about integrity in peace; it is revealed in conflict. A man of God understands that integrity is closely tied to stewardship. Whether entrusted with time, money, authority, or influence, he manages what God has given him responsibly. He does not misuse resources, abuse power, or pursue selfish ambition. He knows he will give an account to God for how he lived, how he led, and how he loved. Integrity keeps him mindful that everything he has belongs to God, and therefore everything he does matters.

Integrity also provides legacy. Abraham Lincoln, "I am not bound to win, but I am bound to be true. I am not bound to succeed, but I am bound to live by the light I have." A man's integrity outlives him. His children, family, and those he leads will remember not merely what he said, but how he lived. Titles fade, achievements rust, and applause dies down, but integrity leaves a lasting imprint. A man of God desires to finish well, knowing that faithfulness over a lifetime speaks louder than moments of success. He understands that one act of compromise can undo years of credibility, but consistent integrity builds a legacy that honors God. Ultimately, a man of God walks in integrity because he walks with God. G. K. Chesterton, "Morality, like art, consists in drawing a line somewhere." The closer a man walks with God, the less comfortable he becomes with compromise. He lives with an awareness of God's presence, knowing that every step, every decision, and every hidden thought is before Him.

A man of God who walks in integrity stands firm in a shifting world. He may not always be understood, praised, or rewarded by men, but he is approved by God. And in the end, that approval is all that truly matters. Billy Graham, "Integrity is the glue that holds our way of life together." There is too much compromise in the world today. Too many people are dishonest and don't keep their word. They then wonder why they can't get ahead in life. The answer is simple. It's because they don't have integrity. Integrity is the foundation a successful life is built on. Be honest, be trustworthy, be a person of your word. Be the man God called you to be. You can have talent, vision, and a truckload of determination. But without integrity, you'll never reach your full potential. When you have integrity, you pay your bills on time, and you keep your commitments. You don't buy things you know you can't pay for. A real man is a man who walks with integrity. He's a man who does the right thing when no one is watching.

Men with integrity are not afraid of what others may find out about them, because their lives are consistent in public and in private. When you walk in the light of integrity, there are no shadows, no double standards, and nothing to hide. Integrity removes the fear of exposure and replaces it with peace of mind. The character of a man of integrity is rooted in truth, not appearances or approval. Such a man stands confident and unashamed, knowing that honesty is both his shield in adversity and his strength in every season of life. Integrity is the first step to true greatness. Always ask yourself, "What is the right thing to do?" There are ten elements that make up personal integrity, and the Bible lists different people who are examples of these qualities. The ten elements are honesty (Daniel), compassion (Boaz), wisdom (Solomon), self-control (Timothy), joy (Paul). Trust (Abraham), faithfulness (Caleb and Joshua), balance (Mary and Martha), sexual purity (Joseph), and endurance (Job).

The Greek word for "integrity" is "integer" and it means 'whole, complete, one.' It refers to a whole number and not a fraction. Just as we talk about a whole number, we also talk about a person who is undivided. A man of integrity lives rightly, is not divided, is not a different person in different circumstances. He is not like a weathervane that changes direction with every shift of social winds. He is the same person in private that he is in public. In other words, what you see is what you get. Don't treat people at work nice and kind and then go home and be rude to your family. Don't be loving in public and hateful in private. That's not integrity, that's hypocrisy. You should treat your family better than you treat anyone else. Be consistent. Be the same on Monday as you are in church on Sunday. Be the same at work as you are at home. You're not being asked to be perfect, you're being asked to be real. Authenticity is what God can shape, strengthen, and use so stop pretending you're somebody you're not.

Live a life of wholeness, a life that isn't divide into different compartments or categories. In other words, don't act one way at church and another way at home and at work. You are a whole person and act the same no matter where you're at. That's integrity. You don't wear a mask, and you don't pretend. Be authentic. Be real. Don't be a fake. Don't be a phony.

Don't be somebody you're not. Don't copycat the behavior of someone else. Be you. Be the person God created you to be. Jesus said of Nathanael, "Now here is a genuine son of Israel, a man of complete integrity" (John 1:47). Nathanael was a man in whom there was no deceit. He was an upright, honest man who was free from hypocrisy and double standards. Every real man should be like that, a man of integrity with high standards and a moral character. Live in such a way that Jesus will describe you the same way He described Nathanael. Be a man if integrity and let it be said there is no deceit or hypocrisy in you.

1 Sam. 16:7, "Man looks at the outward appearance, but the Lord looks at the heart." Men whose hearts are pure and whose motives are clean create a dwelling place for the presence of God in their lives. Men who walk in integrity align their actions with truth, opening their hearts to hear God clearly and follow Him faithfully. Where purity and integrity remain steadfast, the nearness, favor, and guidance of God are experienced daily. Those who walk closely with God will feel His power at work within them, strengthening and guiding every step. As they surrender their hearts to Him, clarity replaces confusion and His voice becomes unmistakable. In His presence, they will know the purpose of God for their life and walk in it with confidence and peace. They will dwell in the unshakable peace of God and fully experience the life-giving pardon of God. These are the men who are called the friends of God. And it all starts with integrity, with who you are when no one else is looking.

Many men are concerned about their image, but God is concerned about their integrity. Most men work hard to protect how they are seen by others, but God looks beyond appearances to the truth of who they are. Image may impress people, but integrity is what honors God and builds a life that truly stands firm. Men often labor to protect their reputation - how they are seen by others - but God searches the heart and measures the truth of who they really are. Reputation is built in public, but character is forged in private, and God values what remains faithful when no one is watching. Prov. 3:22 (NLT), "The Lord hates people with twisted hearts, but He delights in those who have integrity." Reputation is what people think you are shaped by opinions, appearances, and moments others see. Integrity is who you really are when no one is watching, formed by your values, choices, and obedience to what is right. Protect your integrity, because it builds a reputation that time, truth, and God Himself will defend.

A real man of God knows that integrity must be one of his highest values. He understands that integrity is a sacred commitment to live truthfully before God and others, even when no one is watching. His character is proven not by words alone, but by consistent obedience, honesty, and faithfulness in every season of life. Integrity demands that every area of your life - public and private, seen and unseen - is lived with the same unwavering intensity and commitment to what is right. You'll demand excellence in your marriage, the same way you do with your career. How do you become a person of integrity? A good place to start is by keeping all your promises. People of integrity keep their word. They do what they say they're going to do. They understand that trust is built not by intentions, but by follow-through, so they do what they say they are going to do. Their consistency between words and actions becomes a quiet testimony of their character, earning respect and confidence from God and from others.

Prov. 25:14, "A person who promises a gift but doesn't give it is like clouds and wind that bring no rain." A man who does not keep his word erodes the very foundation of his character. Words spoken without follow-through are nothing more than hot air - loud, impressive for a moment, but empty and powerless when tested. Such a man may promise much, but delivers little, revealing a life without weight, depth, or substance. Integrity is what gives a man credibility; without it, his words carry no value, his commitments mean nothing, and his influence fades. A man's worth is not measured by how boldly he speaks, but by how faithfully he stands behind what he says, even when it costs him something. Broken promises are the number one cause of bitterness in children. Keep your promises even when it hurts. Make a pledge to be a man of complete integrity in every situation with your whole heart. Act like a man and live with integrity in your relationships, at work, in your community, and at church.

Men of integrity pay their bills. They understand that paying their bills is a test of their integrity and a reflection of their character. Financial integrity means honoring commitments, living within your means, and taking responsibility for the resources entrusted to you. The way a man manages his money reveals his discipline, honesty, and respect for others, because every bill paid on time declares, "My word matters." True integrity shows up not only in public faith and strong talk, but in private financial decisions where no one else is watching. A lack of integrity is revealed when a person consistently spends more than they make, choosing immediate gratification over responsibility and discipline. Ps. 37:21 says, "The wicked man borrows and never pays back." Living beyond one's means creates bondage, erodes trust, and places unnecessary burdens on others, while integrity calls us to live within our limits, honor our commitments, and steward wisely what God has entrusted to us.

You become a person of integrity by refusing to gossip. This is relational integrity. Don't talk bad about people behind their back. Don't listen to gossip either. Every time you gossip, you lose integrity. Prov. 11:13 (MSG), "A gossip can't be trusted with a secret, but someone of integrity won't violate a confidence." The world today needs men of integrity who know how to keep a secret. Prov. 10:18, "Anyone who spreads gossip is a fool." You become a person of integrity by doing your best at work. This is vocational integrity. Christian men should be the best workers in the whole company. Why? Because they work with integrity. They put in the extra effort. They go the extra mile. They show up on time, stay focused, and don't waste the day on long breaks, proving that discipline and consistency separate those who succeed from those who fail. Col. 3:23 (NLT), "Work hard and cheerfully at what you do, as though you were working for the Lord rather than for people."

One of the greatest blessings of walking in integrity is the deep personal confidence and stability it produces in your life. When your words, actions, and values are aligned, there is no inner conflict or hidden fear of being exposed. You can stand firmly on who you are. Integrity removes confusion and double-mindedness, giving you clarity of purpose and direction. You know where you stand, what you believe, and why you move the way you do. As a result, you walk with steady confidence, make sound decisions, and move forward without hesitation, knowing exactly who you are and where you're going. Prov. 10:9 (NLT), "People with integrity have a firm footing, but those who follow crooked paths will slip and fall." When you have integrity, you're standing on solid ground. Prov. 11:3 (MSG), "The integrity of the honest keeps them on track." Another blessing of integrity is a lasting legacy. Your character will be transferred into the people around you. It will go on from generation to generation.

One of the greatest blessings of integrity are the rewards you'll receive in eternity. Eternal blessings are the greatest blessings of all because they do not fade with time or circumstance. While earthly rewards are temporary, eternal blessings are secured by God and endure forever and ever. When you set your heart on what is eternal, you gain a hope and inheritance that can never be taken away. Matt. 25:21, "Well done! You are a good and trusted servant! Because you were faithful with small things, I'll now put you in charge of much greater things." Notice the word "small." That's where the rewards are. It's in the small moments that you show real integrity. People may applaud the big moments in your life yet overlook the quiet acts of faithfulness you practice every day. Even when no one else notices, God sees every small thing you do and honors it. Walking in integrity in the small things will change your life now and in eternity to come. That's the power of integrity.

| 22 |

"THE COMMITTED LIFE"

It is time for all men to rise up and be the men God called them to be. Now is the moment to lead with integrity, serve with purpose, and walk boldly in the calling God has placed on your life. It's time to act like a man by embracing biblical masculinity marked by courage, responsibility, humility, and sacrificial love that honors God. True manhood is not about dominance or pride, but about standing firm in faith and living in obedience to God's calling. God created you to know Him deeply, not casually, and to walk in a committed relationship that shapes every part of your life. His purpose for you is to lead with conviction and reflect God's character through bold obedience every day. If you're going to do anything well, you must be fully committed to it. Half-hearted effort produces half-finished results, but wholehearted commitment releases discipline, consistency, and growth. What you give yourself to completely is what ultimately shapes your success and your legacy.

The committed life is not easy, because obedience to God often requires sacrifice, discipline, and perseverance. Yet it is the very life God has called you to - a path shaped by purpose, growth, and unwavering faith. What costs you comfort today will reward you with strength, peace, and eternal impact tomorrow. It's a life marked by unwavering confidence in Jesus trusting His promises, walking in His truth, and standing firm no matter the circumstances. You have the utmost confidence that "all things work together for good to those who love God" (Rom. 8:28). You can make the commitment to act like a man because you know the Spirit of Jesus Christ is at work in your life (Phil. 1:19). The committed life is guided by the fact that God is honored by your life and the things you do. 1 Cor. 6:20 says, "God bought you with a high price. So you must honor God with your body." When you act like a man, God receives glory and honor. There is no better reason to commit yourself to being a real man of God.

Paul wrote in Phil. 1:21, "For to me, to live is Christ, and die is gain." That's commitment. To act like a man is to live a life wholly surrendered to Christ, where every breath is devoted to His purpose. To live meant fruitful service for Jesus, and to die meant a glorious gain in His presence. There was no loss either way. That kind of resolve is true commitment; a faith so anchored in Christ that even death becomes victory. Paul's life was guided by these words. It's what caused him to make the commitment to act like a man by living boldly and finishing his race with unwavering commitment to Christ. Let these words of Paul be your mission statement. Let them be the compass for your life that tells you where your time and energy need to go. Living for Christ should be the compass for your life, setting the direction for every step you take and every decision you face. When He is your true Lord, His will guides you to make the commitments that shape your character, your priorities, and your purpose.

A committed life is fueled by the unshakable conviction that your labor is not in vain and that fruit will come in due season. This belief sustains you through unseen progress, quiet obedience, and moments when results seem delayed. When conviction anchors your heart, perseverance becomes natural because you trust that faithfulness will always produce a harvest. Paul said in Phil. 1:22 (NLT), "But if I live, I can do more fruitful work for Christ." When you are fully committed to act like a man, you'll put the plan of God and the needs of others above your own wants and desires. God's agenda always takes precedence over your agenda. Committing to God's plan gives you a purpose for living, a reason to act like a man. Eph. 2:10 says, "We are His workmanship, created in Christ Jesus for good works." When you stay committed, you give God room to work through you to bless, strengthen, and uplift the lives of others. Life doesn't get any better than being used by Him to make a real difference.

When you commit to act like a man you align your life with God's design for strength and leadership. That commitment produces divine freedom, breaking the chains of fear, passivity, and compromise that limit your potential. Walking in that freedom empowers you to pursue greater accomplishments with confidence, purpose, and lasting impact. Vince Lombardi said, "The quality of each man's life is the full measure of that man's commitment to excellence and victory." Doing great things takes great commitment. You cannot keep all your options open and still give yourself fully to the mission. You can't have one foot in and one foot out and expect good things to happen. True commitment requires focus, sacrifice, and the courage to close the door on distractions so you can walk boldly into God's purpose. Commitment is not a half-hearted effort; it demands your whole heart, mind, and strength. To be a real man of God, you must be fully surrendered and unwavering in your actions, choices, and obedience.

God wants a commitment from you based on who He is, what He told you to do, and what you will do in light of that information. When you commit to acting like a man, it shows up in your words, your actions, and the way you carry responsibility. True manhood is revealed in daily decisions, in choosing integrity over convenience, courage over comfort, and discipline over excuses. Over time, those consistent choices shape your character and leave a visible mark on everyone around you. Your decisions reveal what you truly believe, but your actions Your actions demonstrate whether those decisions are authentic. Commitment to act like a man is not measured by words or intentions, but by the consistent choices you make and the discipline to follow through. Let it be known that making a commitment will cost you something. It takes obligation, determination, and discipline. Jesus said, "If anyone desires to come after Me, let him deny himself, and take up his cross, and follow Me" (Matt. 16:24).

Great men are not born extraordinary; they are ordinary men who choose to commit themselves to something far greater than personal comfort or gain. Their greatness is forged through sacrifice, discipline, and unwavering dedication to a cause bigger than their own name. In that commitment, purpose rises, character is refined, and legacy is formed. Nothing shapes your life more than the commitments you choose to make, because they determine what you say yes to and what you must say no to. When your commitments align with your values and purpose, they become the foundation that directs your time, energy, and future. The truth is, you become what you are committed to. Commitment reveals your values by exposing what truly matters to you when choices must be made. What you consistently invest your time, energy, and loyalty in shows what you believe is important. In the end, your commitments clearly declare what you value most and what you genuinely love.

With commitment comes loyalty, reliability, and being devoted. It means to pledge allegiance to something or someone. A great example of commitment is found in the words Ruth spoke to her mother-in-law Naomi. She said, "For wherever you go, I will go; And wherever you lodge, I will lodge. Your people shall be my people, and your God, my God" (Ruth 1:16). True commitment is revealed through involvement. It's when you show up, engage, and invest yourself in what you say matters. If you're not involved, your commitment remains words, not action. Commit to look for opportunities to put your talents and abilities to work, opportunities that allow you to act like a man. Once you choose your commitments, your character follows because what you commit to consistently shapes who you become. This is why you need to choose your commitments carefully. Your destiny is determined by the commitments you make. Not only do they determine your present destiny, but your eternal destiny as well.

Nothing great happens in life without making commitments, because commitment is the force that moves good intentions into meaningful action. When you commit, you choose a direction, and that choice gives your life focus, purpose, and momentum. Commitments clarify what truly matters to you, shaping your priorities and guiding your daily decisions. They anchor you when challenges arise, keeping you steady when obstacles appear. Without commitment, potential remains unused and dreams stay distant, but with it, effort gains meaning and progress becomes inevitable. Commitment will transform ordinary days into a purposeful journey, turning vision into reality and leading your life toward lasting significance. Commitment causes you to accomplish great things. It's not easy but it's worth all the hard work that goes into it. When you faithfully serve your commitments with consistency and integrity, they will eventually return the favor by advancing your purpose and carrying your cause forward.

Prov. 16:3, "Commit your works to the Lord and your plans will be established." The Message Bible says, "Put God in charge of your work, then what you've planned will take place." The Hebrew word for "commit" literally means 'to roll.' When you commit your work to the Lord, you completely roll everything over to Him. You intentionally place every plan, burden, and outcome into His hands. It is a full surrender trusting that He directs your efforts, corrects your course, and carries what you cannot. In doing so, you find peace, confidence, and strength knowing the results rest with Him, not you. When you make a commitment to act like a man, God honors that decision and blesses your efforts according to His perfect will. As you walk in strength, integrity, and obedience, His favor aligns your steps with His purpose and timing. You are to commit yourself to serve the Lord faithfully and leave the results to Him. Have faith that God is working for His ultimate good through your commitment to please Him daily.

You must commit yourself to act like a man of God and all the things that go with it. The truth is, you can't have a worthy life without making some kind of commitment, because commitment is what gives your days direction, meaning, and weight. A life without commitment drifts aimlessly, but a committed life is anchored to purpose and guided by conviction. When you choose to make a commitment to God, to your values, to your calling, and to doing what is right, you step into responsibility, growth, and sacrifice, all of which shape character and produce lasting impact. Commitment demands something of you, but it also gives something back: a life that matters, a legacy that endures, and the deep satisfaction of knowing you lived intentionally rather than by accident. Commitments define your life, shaping the direction, character, and outcome of everything you pursue so the key is to make good ones that align with truth and purpose. It all starts, of course, with a commitment to God.

Rom. 6:13 (NLT), "Give yourselves completely to God. Use your whole body as an instrument to do what is right for the glory of God." The Message Bible says, "Throw yourselves wholeheartedly and fulltime into God's way of doing things." That's the highest commitment you can make in life. Rom. 12:1 (NCV), "Offer your lives as a living sacrifice to Him. Your offering must be only for God and pleasing to Him." The duty of every man is to commit to God. He has a great purpose for your life, but it will be worthless unless you commit to it. The world needs committed and dedicated men of honor who love God with unwavering faithfulness. There are five things God wants to do with your life. He wants you to know Him, love Him, grow in Him, serve Him, and share Him with others. Act like a man and commit to doing these five things. What is a man? He's a nobody who tells anybody about a Somebody who loves everybody. Do that and you'll be a real man through whom God can do great things.

Masculine energy, when surrendered to God, is not about dominance or ego but about commitment, courage, and responsibility. You are called to channel your strength with purpose - to stand firm in truth, to protect what is sacred, and to lead with humility and conviction. God-honoring masculinity shows up in faithful commitment when walking away would be easier, and in courageous obedience when fear tempts you to retreat. It is the resolve to act rightly even when no one is watching, to serve rather than seek status, and to lay down selfish ambition in favor of God's will. When your masculine energy is anchored in commitment and guided by courage, it becomes a force that builds, restores, and glorifies God through a life lived with integrity and unwavering faith. Men who never reach their full potential are often men who never fully commit to purpose, discipline, or growth. A divided heart produces a diminished life, but commitment unlocks the strength to become all a man was created to be.

Luke 9:59,60 tells how Jesus said to a man, "Follow Me." The man replied, "Lord, let me first go and bury my father." The man lacked full commitment. Partial commitment is no commitment. It keeps you back from your greater purpose. You need to be fully and completely committed to God and what He has called you to do, which is to act like a man. This is why you need to commit to yourself. Don't neglect yourself. You have the responsibility to improve your life. Jude 20,21, "Build yourselves up in your most holy faith and pray in the Holy Spirit. Keep yourselves in the love of God." Become a better person, a better man. Take care of yourself. Take care of your spirit, soul, and body. It's not your pastor's job to build you up, it's your job. Stop asking people to pray for you all the time. Go to God and pray yourself. Throw yourself wholeheartedly into becoming the man God is shaping you to be, and you will be amazed at the miraculous work He accomplishes both within you and through your life.

You need to align your God-given masculinity with the God-given purpose for your life because masculinity was never meant to exist without direction. Strength without purpose becomes pride, aggression, or selfish ambition, but strength submitted to God becomes power that builds, protects, and serves. God designed masculinity to be anchored in responsibility, courage, discipline, and sacrificial love, in qualities that find their fullest expression when a man walks in obedience to his calling. When your identity as a man is shaped by God's truth rather than culture's confusion, your strength is refined, your passions are focused, and your life produces lasting fruit. True masculinity is not about dominance or image; it is about alignment and standing firmly in who God created you to be and faithfully pursuing what He created you to do. Being a real man requires commitment. Life is not easy and shortcuts come with consequences. You need to be committed to your role as a man until the end.

Always make decisions with the end in mind. Before you do anything, think about the future. Think about the next generation. Potiphar's wife could have easily had Joseph promoted but he chose not to take the easy way out. He was committed to a cause. When tempted by Potiphar's wife he said, "How then can I do this great wickedness and sin against God?" (Gen. 39:9). Always face life head-on, knowing that strength is forged in challenge, not comfort. The easy way may promise relief, but it rarely produces growth, character, or lasting reward. Stand firm, press forward, and embrace the hard path for it's the one that shapes you into who you're meant to become. Be like Caleb who was committed at the age of eighty-five. He told Joshua to give him his mountain, and he would take it (Josh. 14:10-12). To act like a man takes a life-long commitment. You must be forever pressing forward with unwavering faith and discipline toward the goal of being the man God called you to be.

Nobody is naturally great. We're just normal, ordinary men. We become great when we commit to something greater than ourselves because true greatness is never born out of self-interest alone. When our lives are anchored to a higher purpose - serving God, helping others, building legacy, or advancing truth - we are lifted beyond comfort and selfish ambition. In giving ourselves to something eternal, meaningful, and sacrificial, we discover strength we didn't know we had, and our lives begin to leave an impact that outlives us. David faced Goliath because he was committed to a cause. He asked his brother, "Is there not a cause?" (1 Sam. 17:19). Daniel refused to defile himself with the king's delicacies because he was committed to a cause (Dan. 1:8). We all need a cause bigger than ourselves to live for. Living only for yourself is not a good enough reason to get out of bed in the morning. If you don't commit to a cause, you become nothing in life and should just stay in bed and not get up.

An uncommitted life drifts without purpose because when nothing is important, nothing is worth sacrificing for. It causes you to live a selfish life because without commitment, the heart naturally turns inward, placing personal comfort above responsibility, calling, and service to others. True meaning is found when you commit to something greater than yourself, allowing purpose to replace selfishness and direction to replace emptiness. You need something bigger than yourself to live for. This draws you out of yourself and makes you bigger than yourself. Committing to a cause bigger than yourself pulls you beyond comfort and self-interest, awakening purpose, courage, and discipline you didn't know you had. True greatness is revealed when your life is spent serving something eternal, meaningful, and far greater than personal gain. Commit yourself to acting like a man and allow God to be the guiding force in your life. And always remember, you become what you're committed to.

| 23 |

"GOD'S OWN HEART"

To act like a man in the way God defines it, like David, you must first become a man after God's own heart. David's strength was not rooted in pride, position, or outward appearance, but in his deep love for God, his humility, and his willingness to obey even when it was costly. A man after God's heart seeks God in private before standing boldly in public, repents quickly when he falls, and trusts the Lord more than his own abilities. True manhood is formed not by dominance or self-promotion, but by devotion, courage, integrity, and an unshakable dependence on God. 1 Sam. 16:7, "For the Lord does not see as man sees; for man looks at the outward appearance, but the Lord looks at the heart." God knows what lies in the deepest chambers of your heart - every thought, motive, and hidden desire. He knows what makes you tick, what drives you when no one else is watching, and what shapes your choices. He knows your character completely, not just who you appear to be, but the person you truly are.

David loved God so much that the reason he faced Goliath was "that all the earth may know that there is a God in Israel" (1 Sam. 16:46). David was a man of godly character whose heart was fully devoted to the Lord, and he consistently chose what was right even when it cost him personally. He stood firmly for justice and truth, trusting God to defend him as he walked in integrity and obedience. He could not stand the fact that Goliath had defied the living God of Israel. This is where he drew the line. He faced the giant without intimidation. Vs. 48 says David "ran toward the army to meet the Philistine." He ran toward the problem, not away from it. Why? Because he was a man after God's own heart and Goliath had just defied his God. David was bold and aggressive. He had grit and courage to face the enemy. He was faithful to the Lord. He had a godly character, viewing every situation through God's eyes and choosing faith, righteousness, and obedience above all else.

David missed the mark many times, yet his heart remained steadfastly devoted to God. Even in failure, he continually turned back to the Lord with humility, repentance, and trust. The Psalms reveal a deep, passionate love for God, showing that David's greatest strength was not perfection, but unwavering devotion. His close relationship with the Lord was the wellspring of his faith, courage, and unwavering confidence. Because he trusted God intimately, he faced opposition not with fear, but with bold assurance that the Lord was with him. His strength did not come from his own ability, but from a deep dependence on God who never failed him. Rom. 8:37, "In all these things we are more than conquerors through Him who loved us." David said of the Lord, "He is my refuge and my fortress; My God, in Him I will trust" (Ps. 91:2). Trust is not a feeling you wait for - it's an action you choose. When you trust God, you move forward in obedience, stepping out in faith even when emotions are uncertain.

Does your life truly reflect that you trust God, or is your trust only expressed in words? Genuine faith takes bold, obedient steps and is willing to risk comfort and security to follow God's call. Those who truly trust Him do not run from the battle - they stand firm, knowing God fights with them. When you trust God, courage rises within you and you step into battle with fearless, tenacious determination. Faith turns ordinary obedience into heroic action, empowering you to stand firm when others retreat. With God as your strength, you don't just survive the fight - you advance boldly and overcome. It's what causes you to stand your ground and fight s good fight. It's what causes you to be victorious in battle. God is not searching for ability or perfection - He is looking for men after His own heart, men who trust Him enough to obey and pursue Him fully. These are men who keep moving forward in faith, refusing to retreat no matter what opposition, hardship, or battle stands in their way.

To understand why David was a man after God's own heart, it is necessary to see what characteristics he had to qualify for such an exalted position. God said in Acts 13:22, "I have found David son of Jesse, a man after My own heart; he will do everything I want him to do." To be considered a man after God's own heart, you must be willing to surrender your will to His and obey Him fully without conditions, excuses, or delay. This kind of man does not merely admire God's ways or agree with His commands in theory; he lives them out in practice, even when obedience is costly, uncomfortable, or misunderstood. He seeks God's direction above his own desires, choosing faithfulness over convenience and righteousness over recognition. Like a true servant, he understands that obedience is not about perfection, but about a heart posture that says, "Lord, whatever You want me to do, I will do it." When a man aligns his actions with God's will, he proves that his heart truly belongs to God.

When God takes the measure of a man, He does not put a tape measure around his mind to see how much he knows. He puts it around his heart to see how much he obeys. 1 Sam. 15:22 says, "Behold, to obey is better than sacrifice." When the Bible says David was a man after God's own heart, it reveals that his greatness was not rooted in perfection, but in a life consistently marked by obedience, repentance, and a sincere desire to follow God's will above his own. In 1 Sam. 13 the prophet Samuel confronted Saul for disobeying the word of the Lord. He said, "You have done foolishly. You have not kept the commandment of the Lord your God what He commanded you. But now your kingdom shall not continue. The Lord has sought for Himself a man after His own heart" (vs. 13,14). Saul was not a man after God's own heart because he repeatedly chose disobedience, while David was called a man after God's own heart because, despite his failures, he humbled himself and obeyed God's will.

David was far from perfect. He failed, stumbled, and bore the weight of serious mistakes just like any other man. What set him apart was not flawlessness, but a heart that consistently turned back toward God in humility, repentance, and trust. His life reminds us that God is not searching for perfect people, but for willing hearts that pursue Him above all else. David's deepest desire was to do the will of God, and he set his heart on obedience rather than self-promotion. He sought the Lord's direction, trusted God's timing, and aligned his actions with God's purposes. In sharp contrast, Saul's heart drifted into rebellion, choosing partial obedience and personal control over wholehearted submission to God. David's deepest desire was to do the will of God. He set his heart to obey God in contrast to Saul's heart of rebellion. This is why God removed Saul from being king and raised up David to take his place. To be a man after God's own heart, you have to love God with all your heart and soul.

Love and obedience in the Bible are inseparably connected, revealing that true love for God is demonstrated through faithful action. Jesus makes this clear in John 14:15 when He says, "If you love Me, you will keep My commands," showing that obedience is the natural expression of genuine love. Your willingness to follow His instructions reflects not obligation, but a heart transformed by love. Love is the underlying foundation for obedience. If you struggle with obeying God, it often reveals a deeper struggle in fully loving and trusting Him. True love for God moves beyond words and emotions and shows itself through willing submission to His will. As your love for Him grows, obedience becomes less of a burden and more of a joyful response to who He is. David obeyed God better than Saul because he loved God more than Saul. Saul was always pointing to himself while David was always pointing to God. Saul wanted the people to look at him; David wanted the people to look at God.

David was a special man, so special that he is the only person in the Bible called "a man after God's own heart." This was not because he was perfect, but because he deeply loved God, trusted Him fully, and was quick to repent when he failed. David's life shows us that God values a sincere, humble heart that seeks Him above all else. David was faithful and loyal in heart, serving God with unwavering dedication. Because of this steadfast devotion, God chose David to be king over all of Israel, exalting a servant whose trust was fully anchored in Him. As a young lad he was responsible for taking care of his father's sheep, and he performed his duties faithfully and diligently. You can't expect God to use you significantly in His kingdom until you are first dedicated in whatever work you are presently doing. God is continually seeking faithful, caring men who will shepherd His children, carry out His divine plans, and make the world better through obedient hearts and righteous leadership.

Talk is easy and words are cheap, but faith is proven through consistent, obedient action. When your life aligns with what you profess, your faithful actions become signposts pointing toward a glorious, God-ordained future. If you are faithful and diligent like David, your eyes will remain open to recognize opportunities that others overlook. Faithfulness sharpens your vision, positioning you to serve, give, and lead with purpose. When your heart is aligned with God, He will use your diligence to make you a continual blessing to others. A responsible man actively looks for ways to make things better and more productive. He understands that stewardship means adding value wherever he is planted, whether in his work, family, or community. True responsibility is revealed in a man's commitment to growth, progress, and positive change. God is naturally attracted to those that love to add value to the world around them. Act like a man and always be found adding value to your family, church, and community.

David is called a man after God's own heart because his life was anchored in absolute faith in God rather than in his own strength or understanding. He consistently trusted God as his defender, provider, and guide. Even when he failed, his faith drew him back to God in genuine repentance, humility, and dependence, revealing a heart that sought God above all else. His unwavering confidence in God's character and promises defined his legacy and set him apart as a man who lived not by sight, but by faith. No place in the Bible illustrates this point better than 1 Sam. 17 which tells how David bravely confronted the giant Goliath. When he was still a young shepherd boy, he had a firm conviction that God was worthy of his trust and confidence. He said, "The Lord who delivered me from the paw of the lion and from the paw of the bear will deliver me from the hand of this Philistine" (vs. 37). David had a faith that pleased God (Heb. 11:6). He knew early on in life that God was to be trusted and obeyed.

David lived with a deep, unwavering awareness that God was fully in control of his life, and this confidence shaped every decision he made. Rather than being paralyzed by fear in the face of impending danger, he placed his trust in the Lord's sovereignty, believing that his life rested securely in God's hands. This faith allowed David to move forward with courage and peace, knowing that the same God who guided and anointed him would also deliver him from every threat. Whether facing enemies, uncertainty, or adversity, David's assurance was not in his own strength but in the faithfulness and power of God to protect and preserve him. How else could he venture into a potentially fatal situation with such calm and confidence? God was pleased by David's faith and rewarded him for his faithfulness and trust in Him. David slew the giant, had songs written about him, and later because the greatest king in the history of Israel. May all men be found with the same heart he had.

David was a man after God's own heart because gratitude flowed naturally from his relationship with the Lord. He understood that every victory, every provision, and every breath of life came from God's gracious hand, and he never took those blessings for granted. Whether he was tending sheep, fleeing from enemies, or reigning as king, David consistently paused to thank the Lord for His faithfulness. His psalms overflow with praise, revealing a heart that never forgot God in moments of triumph or seasons of trial. Whether lifted by victory or bowed by hardship, he consistently turned his gratitude toward the Lord, acknowledging Him as the source of every blessing. David's thankfulness kept him humble, anchored his trust in God rather than in his own strength, and reflected a deep awareness that all he had and all he had come from the Lord alone. Ps. 100:4 says, "Enter into His gates with thanksgiving, and into His courts with praise. Be thankful to Him and bless His name."

David loved God's law, delighting in it as a treasure that guided his steps and shaped his heart. He didn't see God's commands as a burden, but as a source of life, wisdom, and joy that kept him close to the Lord in every season. Ps. 119:47,48 says, "And I delight myself in Your commandments, which I love. My hands also I will lift up to Your commandments, which I love, and I will meditate on Your statutes." It is not hard to see the writer's complete adoration for God's Word. Notice how he meditates on God's statutes. "Blessed are they who keep His statutes and seek Him with all their heart. They do nothing wrong, they walk in His ways" (Ps. 119:2,3). David longed for closeness to God. He said in Ps. 23:6, "I will dwell in the house of the Lord forever." David was not perfect. He was flawed and made many mistakes. Still, Jesus identified Himself with him. Jesus is called the Son of David and He was born in Bethlehem just as David was, establishing Him as the rightful Messiah and King.

David's example provides a powerful roadmap for how we are to live our lives and how we are to act like men. He was not defined by perfection, but by a relentless pursuit of God's heart. David showed courage when others shrank back, faith when circumstances looked impossible, and humility when correction was needed. He understood that true strength begins in private obedience long before it is displayed in public victory. As a man, David teaches us to trust God in the field before facing giants, to lead with integrity rather than ego, and to repent quickly when we fall. His life reminds us that biblical manhood is not about dominance or image, but about devotion, responsibility, courage, and wholehearted dependence on God. He was a humble man. Ps. 62:9, "Surely men of low degree are a vapor, men of high degree are a lie. If they are weighed in the balances, they are altogether lighter than vapor." He was reverent. Ps. 18:3, "I will call upon the Lord, who is worthy to be praised."

He gave God recognition by praising Him with his whole heart and openly declaring God's wondrous works, showing that true strength begins with grateful, vocal worship. He was obedient because he sought understanding from God, knowing that true obedience flows from a surrendered and teachable heart. As Psalm 119:34 declares, "Give me understanding, and I will keep your law and obey it with all my heart," showing that obedience is not forced, but born out of love and devotion to God. He trusted God, knowing that when the Lord is your light and salvation, fear has no place to dwell. With God as the strength of his life, he stood confident and unafraid, resting fully in His power and protection. Ps. 27:1, "The Lord is my light and my salvation; Whom shall I fear? The Lord is the strength of my life; Of whom shall I be afraid?" He loved God with all his heart and soul, and he was repentant when he sinned. Ps. 25:11 says, "For the sake of Your name, O Lord, forgive my iniquity, though it is great."

In order to act like a man, you must first be a man after God's own heart. David was such a man. Next to Jesus, there is more written about David in the Bible than any other person. There are 66 chapters written about David in the Old Testament and 59 references to him in the New Testament. That alone speaks to the depth and significance of his life. Scripture does not present David as flawless, but as fully human - a shepherd, a warrior, a king, a poet, and a worshiper whose heart continually turned toward God. His story captures towering victories and devastating failures, yet through it all, David remained a man after God's own heart. The Bible records his courage in the face of giants, his humility in repentance, his passion in worship, and his reliance on God rather than on his own strength. David's life shows that God is not looking for perfection, but for a heart that is willing to trust Him, return to Him, and be shaped by Him through every season.

David's life was marked by powerful highs and painful lows, a journey filled with victories, failures, faith, and repentance. He was an outcast and a warrior - once a forgotten shepherd boy, tending sheep in obscurity. Yet God raised him from the fields to the throne, making him the greatest king in the history of Israel, so honored that songs were sung celebrating how God used him mightily. He praised God continually, lifting his voice through music and poetry as an offering of worship. A gifted musician and poet, his life and legacy flow through the bloodline of Jesus, pointing generations to the heart of God. David was a great king. In battle, he was fearless. In wisdom and ruling his kingdom, he was without peer. He was a great warrior but still had a tender heart toward God. He had a deep spiritual life with a strong devotion to his Lord. Because of all this, he became known as a man after God's own heart. May your faith, obedience, and perseverance make it undeniable that the same is said of you.

| 24 |

"ACT LIKE A MAN"

For a Christian man, to "act like a man" is not a call to arrogance, dominance, or bravado, but to mature responsibility under God. Scripture consistently challenges men to grow up spiritually, calling them to move beyond immaturity and step into a life of disciplined faith and godly responsibility. God's Word urges men to stand firm, not swayed by cultural pressures or personal fears, but anchored in truth and unwavering trust in Christ. This strength is not rooted in pride or self-reliance, but in humble obedience - daily choosing to submit to Christ's authority and live out His commands. True biblical courage is revealed when a man obeys God even when it is costly, leads with integrity, loves sacrificially, and remains faithful in adversity. In this way, Scripture calls men to a mature, courageous faith that reflects Christ's character and brings honor to God in every area of life. True manhood is not proven by how loud a man speaks, but by a quiet, unwavering faithfulness to God, truth, and responsibility.

Acting like a man begins with submission to God. When a man humbles himself before God, he learns discipline over his impulses, clarity in his decisions, and courage rooted in obedience rather than pride. Submission to God shapes a man's character, teaching him to lead by example, serve with integrity, and stand firm in truth even when it is costly. True manhood is revealed not in self-assertion, but in a willing surrender that allows God to form a man into someone dependable, faithful, and strong for the sake of others. A Christian man understands that true strength is found not in self-assertion, but in surrendering his will to God's greater purpose. This surrender is not weakness; it is the deliberate choice to trust God's wisdom over personal pride. In aligning himself with God's will, he discovers a strength that is steady, enduring, and rooted in divine authority rather than human effort. He understands that authority without submission leads to pride, but submission to God produces stability, clarity, and power.

A Christian man accepts responsibility as a reflection of his faith and his commitment to live under God's authority. He understands that maturity is shown not by shifting blame, making excuses, or avoiding accountability, but by owning his actions, decisions, and their outcomes with humility and integrity. Following the example of Christ, he takes responsibility for his family, his work, his words, and his conduct, recognizing that leadership begins with self-discipline. When he falls short, he does not hide or harden his heart; instead, he repents, learns, and grows stronger through obedience. By accepting responsibility, a Christian man honors God, earns trust from others, and demonstrates a faith that is active, courageous, and grounded in truth. He does not blame others, circumstances, or the past for his failures. He owns his actions, his words, and his decisions. Whether as a husband, father, leader, or servant, he understands that responsibility is not a burden to escape but a calling to embrace.

Acting like a man means standing firm in truth, even when it is uncomfortable, unpopular, or costly. It is the resolve to anchor your life in what is right rather than what is easy, allowing conviction to guide your words, decisions, and actions. A man who stands in truth does not bend to pressure, compromise his values, or shift with every cultural wind; instead, he remains steady, courageous, and dependable. Truth becomes his foundation - shaping his character, strengthening his integrity, and earning the trust of those around him. In standing firm, he reflects maturity, strength, and leadership, proving that real manhood is not measured by power or pride, but by faithfulness to what is right. A Christian man holds fast to God's Word even when it is unpopular, anchoring his life in truth rather than shifting opinions. He understands that faithful obedience endures beyond the moment, knowing God's approval will always outlast the approval and applause of men.

A Christian man exercises self-control by submitting his thoughts, desires, and actions to the lordship of Christ rather than being ruled by impulse or emotion. He understands that true strength is not found in reacting, but in responding with wisdom, restraint, and obedience to God's Word. Through the guidance of the Holy Spirit, he learns to govern his temper, discipline his body, guard his speech, and resist temptation.

Self-control allows him to walk in integrity, lead his family with steadiness, and reflect Christ's character in a world driven by excess and instant gratification. In mastering himself, he honors God, protects his testimony, and proves that spiritual maturity is marked not by domination over others, but by dominion over one's own life. He does not allow his emotions, desires, or impulses to rule him. Strength is shown not by uncontrolled anger or indulgence, but by discipline, restraint, and mastery over the flesh. He understands that real power is the ability to govern oneself.

Acting like a man requires courage - the kind of courage that stands firm when it would be easier to compromise, remain silent, or walk away. It's obedience in the presence of fear, trusting God more than circumstances. True courage is not found in aggression or pride, but in the willingness to do what is right regardless of the cost. It takes courage to accept responsibility, to lead with integrity, and to protect what God has entrusted to you - your faith, your family, and your character. A courageous man faces fear with resolve, resists temptation with strength, and chooses obedience over convenience. In a world that often rewards passivity and excuses weakness, acting like a man means boldly living out truth, conviction, and faith in this dark world. A Christian man is willing to confront sin with truth and courage, not out of pride, but out of love for God and righteousness. He will protect what is right and stand alone if necessary, trusting that obedience to God matters more than the approval of men.

A Christian man walks in humility, fully aware that his strength, wisdom, and success come not from himself but from God. He does not boast in his accomplishments or seek recognition for his service. He knows that everything he has comes from God, and he gladly gives glory where it belongs, never seeking applause for what God alone has done. Humility keeps his strength usable, guarding him from pride and positioning him to serve with integrity. Because his heart remains teachable, he continues to grow, lead, and reflect God's character in every season. He does not seek recognition or control, but willingly submits his heart to the Lord, treating others with grace, patience, and respect. In humility, he listens before he speaks, serves without needing applause, and corrects himself before correcting others. His quiet confidence is rooted in obedience to Christ, knowing that true greatness is found not in being exalted, but in faithfully walking under God's authority.

Acting like a man includes loving sacrificially choosing commitment over convenience and responsibility over comfort. Love, in God's design, is not a fleeting feeling or passive affection, but a deliberate, self-giving commitment that chooses faithfulness, sacrifice, and action for the good of another. It is a love that mirrors Christ's example, willing to give time, strength, pride, and even personal desires for the good of others. This kind of love protects, provides, and perseveres, not because it is easy, but because it is right. A man who loves sacrificially proves his strength not by what he demands, but by what he is willing to give. A Christian man loves not merely with words but with actions that reflect the heart of Christ. He shows up consistently even when love is costly or inconvenient. His faith is proven not by what he says, but by how he lives and stands up for others every day. A godly man lays down his personal preferences choosing instead to serve others selflessly as an expression of Christlike love.

A Christian man is faithful in the unseen places. He understands that integrity is who he is when no one is watching. It is not a performance for applause or a mask worn for approval, but the quiet, unwavering commitment to do what is right simply because it is right. His character is revealed in unseen moments, in choices made without pressure, praise, or recognition. When no eyes are on him, his values still guide his actions, proving that his foundation is firm and his conscience clear. Integrity, for him, is not situational - it is the consistent alignment of his heart, his words, and his deeds, whether in public or in private. His private walk with God matches his public confession of faith, with no contradictions hidden in the shadows. He understands that integrity is proven when no one is watching, and he refuses to wear different faces in different places. His life is whole, undivided, and fully submitted - inside and out - to the truth he proclaims. He knows that consistency honors God and builds trust.

Acting like a man means working diligently, embracing responsibility with consistency, and giving your best effort even when no one is watching. It is the discipline to show up, to labor with integrity, and to understand that excellence honors both God and those who depend on you. A diligent man does not chase shortcuts or excuses; he commits himself fully to the task before him, knowing that faithful work builds character, earns trust, and leaves a lasting legacy. A Christian man values labor as a gift from God, understanding that honest work is a form of worship and obedience. He practices stewardship by faithfully managing his time, talents, and resources for God's glory rather than personal gain alone. Through diligence and responsibility, he reflects Christ by providing for others and leaving what he oversees better than he found it. He gives his best effort, not as a people-pleaser, but as one serving the Lord. He understands that faith does not excuse laziness and that excellence glorifies God.

A Christian man protects rather than exploits because his strength is governed by love, integrity, and reverence for God. He understands that authority is not a license to take advantage of others, but a responsibility to serve, guard, and uplift those entrusted to his care. Whether in his family, workplace, church, or community, he chooses restraint over selfish gain and compassion over control. Guided by Christ's example, he stands as a defender of the vulnerable, honors boundaries, and treats others with dignity and respect. His masculinity is not proven by what he can take, but by what he is willing to safeguard - even at personal cost - reflecting the heart of a true servant-leader. True godly strength is revealed not in domination or control, but in humility, compassion, and the willingness to serve others with love. Whether emotional, spiritual, or physical, his strength becomes a shield for others, not a weapon against them. Protection is one of the clearest expressions of godly masculinity.

Acting like a man involves accountability - the willingness to take responsibility for your actions, decisions, and their outcomes. A man who embraces accountability does not make excuses, shift blame, or hide when things go wrong; instead, he owns his mistakes, learns from them, and corrects his course. Accountability requires integrity, humility, and courage, because it means answering not only to others, but to God and to one's own conscience. When a man holds himself accountable, he builds trust, strengthens his character, and becomes dependable to those who rely on him. True manhood is revealed not by perfection, but by the resolve to stand up, admit fault when necessary, and faithfully carry the weight of responsibility placed on his life. A Christian man welcomes correction and surrounds himself with godly counsel. He does not isolate himself in pride but understands that growth happens in community. Accountability strengthens character and prevents spiritual drift.

A Christian man practices forgiveness as a reflection of the grace he himself has received from God. He understands that forgiveness is not a sign of weakness, but a demonstration of spiritual strength, humility, and obedience to Christ. Rather than holding onto anger, resentment, or the desire for revenge, he chooses to release offenses into God's hands, trusting the Lord to bring justice and healing in His time. Forgiveness allows him to walk in freedom, protects his heart from bitterness, and keeps his relationships rooted in love. By forgiving others, even when it is difficult, a Christian man mirrors the mercy of Christ and becomes a living testimony of the transforming power of God's love. He does not cling to bitterness or rehearse offenses. Knowing how much he has been forgiven, he extends grace freely. Forgiveness is not weakness - it is a powerful declaration that resentment will not rule his heart, but grace, freedom, and strength will.

Acting like a man means persevering through hardship with courage, resolve, and faith. It is standing firm when the pressure is heavy and the path is unclear, choosing endurance over escape and obedience over comfort. True manhood is revealed not in the absence of struggle, but in the willingness to remain faithful when trials test character and refine the heart. A man who perseveres does not quit when life becomes difficult; he presses forward, trusting that God uses adversity to refine faith, deepen character, and produce endurance. Hardship becomes the proving ground where strength is forged, integrity is solidified, and purpose is clarified. Real men don't fold under pressure; they allow adversity to shape their character and refine their resolve. Every trial strengthens their backbone, deepens their discipline, and exposes what truly matters. What was meant to break them instead builds men who stand firm, lead with conviction, and grow stronger through every challenge.

A Christian man leads by example by allowing his life to be a living testimony of his faith in Christ. Rather than relying solely on words, he demonstrates integrity, humility, and strength through his daily actions at home, at work, and in the community. He loves sacrificially, serves willingly, and stands firm in truth even when it is difficult. His leadership is not driven by control or pride, but by obedience to God and a genuine desire to reflect Christ's character. By walking in faith, showing consistency between belief and behavior, and treating others with grace and respect, a Christian man inspires those around him to follow a higher standard and to trust God through his example. True leadership is shown when a man lives out the standards he speaks, not just the words he says. His life becomes a visible testimony of obedience, consistency, and devotion. He does not demand from others what he refuses to practice himself, because integrity begins with example, not authority.

Acting like a man means taking responsibility for what is allowed to shape the heart and mind. A Christian man is intentional about what he allows to shape his thoughts and desires, knowing that what fills his mind will ultimately guide his character, choices, and walk with God. He understands that purity fuels clarity, and that holiness strengthens spiritual authority. A man who walks in strength understands that his thoughts become actions and his affections determine his direction. Guarding the heart requires discernment - refusing bitterness, lust, pride, or fear a place to settle - while guarding the mind means being intentional about what is seen, heard, and believed. This kind of vigilance is not weakness but discipline, a quiet courage that chooses truth over impulse and wisdom over distraction. By protecting his inner life, a man preserves his integrity, strengthens his character, and positions himself to lead, love, and live with purpose and honor.

A Christian man lives with an eternal perspective, measuring his choices not by temporary gain but by lasting impact in God's kingdom. He invests his time, energy, and resources into things that matter to God, knowing that eternity gives meaning to every present choice. He walks with purpose, knowing that faithfulness today echoes into eternity. While the world often applauds quick results, visible rewards, and fleeting recognition, his focus is anchored in what endures beyond the moment. He understands that true success is not found in what can be gained and lost overnight, but in the lives shaped, the character built, and the legacy left behind. Each decision is guided by purpose rather than profit, knowing that seeds planted with faith, integrity, and perseverance may take time to grow but will bear fruit that remains. In this way, success is not counted by what he accumulates, but by the difference he makes quietly, faithfully, and for generations to come.

Ultimately, for a Christian man to "act like a man" is not defined by cultural stereotypes, physical strength, or personal dominance, but by a life that faithfully reflects Christ. Biblical manhood is revealed in Jesus, in His courage to stand for truth, in His humility to serve rather than be served, in His strength expressed through sacrifice, and in His unwavering obedience to the Father. To act like a man is to lead with love, to protect without pride, to remain steadfast under pressure, and to choose righteousness even when it is costly. It is the willingness to lay down one's life - daily, practically, and faithfully - for God, family, and others. In reflecting Christ, a Christian man demonstrates true strength through submission to God, maturity through self-control, and authority through compassion, becoming a living testimony of Christ's character in a broken world. True manhood is not found in cultural stereotypes but in Christlike character that is strong in faith, anchored in truth, and committed to God's purpose. Be that man.

SUMMARY

The command to "act like men" is a call back to God's clear and unchanging standard for biblical manhood found in 1 Cor. 16:13,14. It reminds men to stay spiritually alert, stand firm in the faith, live with courage and strength, and let every action be governed by love. True manhood is not defined by culture, emotion, or convenience, but by conviction, responsibility, and Christlike character. A man who acts like a man watches over his life, remains anchored in truth, accepts responsibility without excuse, and leads with strength tempered by compassion.

This book challenges every man to rise above passivity, reject compromise, and live intentionally for God - strong in faith, steady in character, and faithful in love. The call is clear. The standard is set. Now is the time to act like men. This is not a temporary challenge or a motivational slogan - it is a lifelong commitment to live as God designed. As this book has shown, 1 Cor. 16:13,14 is not merely a verse to be quoted, but a pattern to be lived. It defines a man's posture toward God, toward himself, and toward the world.

To be watchful is to remain spiritually alert in a world filled with distractions and deception. To stand firm in the faith is to live anchored in truth. To be strong is to embrace responsibility. And finally, to do all things with love is to be a blessing to others no matter what the cost may be. "Act Like Men" has not called men to perfection, but to intentional living. It has challenged passivity, exposed compromise, and confronted the lies that have weakened men for generations. It has pointed men back to the timeless standard of God's Word and reminded them that true masculinity is not defined by culture, but by Christ.

The world is watching. Families are depending. The next generation is learning by example. God is calling men to rise, to lead, and to live with conviction. This is the hour for men to take their place - not in pride, but in purpose; not in anger, but in strength governed by love; not in retreat, but in faithful obedience. Stand firm. Be strong. Love well. A real man is bold in faith, strong in character, and grounded in love. As men our calling is to stand, to endure, and to live out our faith openly and courageously. Go into the world, live with conviction, and act like men.

www.ingramcontent.com/pod-product-compliance
Lightning Source LLC
Chambersburg PA
CBHW070908130626
46555CB00001B/55